Finding Your Voice

...you and your government

Lynn A. A. Flaig
Kathryn E. Galvin

Reidmore Books

Acknowledgements

Reidmore Books wishes to thank the following reviewers for their insights and support in the development of this textbook.

Teachers
Alex Newhart, Pine Street School
Sherwood Park, AB

David Powell, McKee Elementary School
Edmonton, AB

Political Scientists
Jane Arscott, Assistant Professor of Political Science and Canadian Studies, University of Alberta

James Lightbody, Professor of Political Science, University of Alberta

Native Content
Linda Laliberte, Executive Director,
Mother Bear Consulting Inc., Edmonton, AB

Credits
Managing editor: Leah-Ann Lymer
Project editor: Carolyn Pogue
Assistant editors: Janet Pinno, David Strand
Design and layout: Leslieanna Blackner Au
Cartography: Wendy Johnson,
    (Johnson Cartographics)
Illustrations: Yu Chao

Reidmore Books Inc.
18228-102 Avenue
Edmonton AB T5S 1S7
tel: 403-444-0912; fax 403-444-0933
toll free: 1-800-661-2859
email: reidmore@compusmart.ab.ca
website: http://www.reidmore.com
printed and bound in Canada

About the Authors

Lynn Flaig is an elementary school principal in Calgary. She received her undergraduate degree in education from the University of Calgary and has a Master's degree from the San Diego State University. She has a broad base of classroom experiences and has been a contributor to the development of numerous teacher resources in social studies.

Kathryn Galvin is currently an elementary school principal in Calgary. Both her Bachelor and Master's degrees in education were received from the University of Calgary. She taught for many years in a range of settings. Ms. Galvin has four years of consulting experience in social studies. She has authored numerous social studies materials, and has contributed to the journal, *History and Social Science Teacher*.

Both authors are known for their responsiveness to the needs of students. Their interesting and informative writing style is conducive to helping students make connections between learning and application in the real world.

Canadian Cataloguing in Publication Data

Flaig, Lynn A.A.
        Finding Your Voice

Includes bibliographical references and index.
ISBN 1-895073-31-6

1. Political participation – Canada – Juvenile literature.
2. Local government – Canada – Juvenile literature.
3. Civics, Canadian – Juvenile literature. I. Galvin, Kathryn E., 1951 - II. Title.

JS1717.A2F52 1997   j323'.042'0971   C97-910415-7

Contents

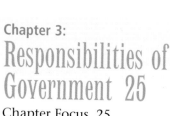

> In Canada, government is a group of elected or appointed citizens, expected to work in the best interests of all people living in our communities, provinces, territories, and country.
>
> —*Kathryn Galvin*

Introduction

In Canada, anyone who is an adult and a Canadian citizen is eligible to vote. Many people feel that voting is the only way to influence how decisions are made by governments. Voting, however, is only one way.

Everyone in Canada has the opportunity to voice an opinion and to influence decisions. For this reason, Canada is called a democratic country.

This book will explain the history of government in Canada and how it works today. Then we will help you recognize opportunities in which you can be involved as a responsible citizen of your community.

Part of being a responsible citizen involves being well informed. As a citizen, you will need to be able to find and interpret many different kinds of information. This book will show you how to use information to ask questions, form opinions, share ideas, and take action.

Our goal is to help you realize the opportunities and the responsibilities you have in Canada, while helping you to gain the skills needed to participate in your government.

Special Features

Each chapter has special elements that will help you to study government in Canada.

➤ Each chapter opens with a Chapter Focus, which consists of a short introduction to the chapter and a list of questions for you to consider as you read.

➤ Following the Chapter Focus is a Vocabulary list that provides definitions for the special words in the chapter. The Vocabulary words are also boldfaced within the chapter, and are listed in the Glossary at the end of this book.

➤ Profile boxes give more detailed information about particular people, places, and events.

➤ Word Origin boxes explain where particular words come from and how they came to be used today.

➤ Your Turn questions and activities occur throughout each chapter after sections of text. These questions and activities help you to use the information that you have just learned.

➤ Power sidebars will explain the concept of power to you. They will also show you how your own personal power can influence decisions made in your community.

➤ Each chapter ends with Ideas activities. Some of these activities assign a research task and describe the research skills needed. Others present a problem for you to offer solutions to.

The Use of BCE and CE

The neutral designations BCE and CE are used in this book. BCE stands for "Before the Common Era" and CE stands for "the Common Era." BCE refers to the same time period as BC, whereas CE refers to the same time period as AD.

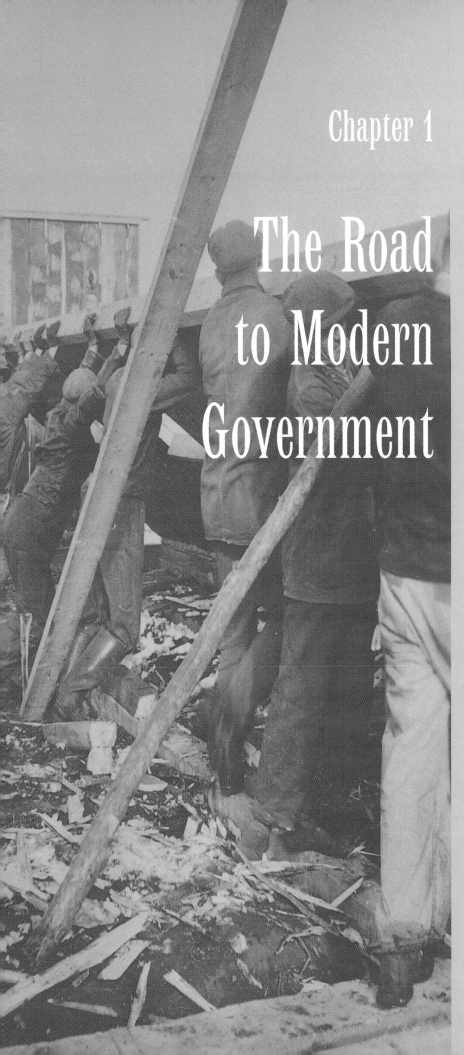

Chapter 1

The Road to Modern Government

Chapter Focus

Have you ever heard of countries where people must do exactly what the leader demands? Not all governments in our modern world are the same. In Canada we are fortunate that people have many freedoms. Making choices is one of those freedoms. Making choices is part of our lifestyle. Because of our democratic system of government, people in Canada have a voice and a vote.

Throughout history, there have been many different styles of government. In this chapter, you will explore three early styles. You will be introduced to early government in China, Greece, and England. As you examine each of these governments, begin comparing and contrasting the ways different groups of people organized to meet their needs.

As you read this chapter, consider these questions:

➤ How did government begin?

➤ Why do we need government?

➤ How did early governments work for people?

➤ What is **power**?

➤ How has government changed through time?

➤ Should all governments be the same?

How Did Government Begin?

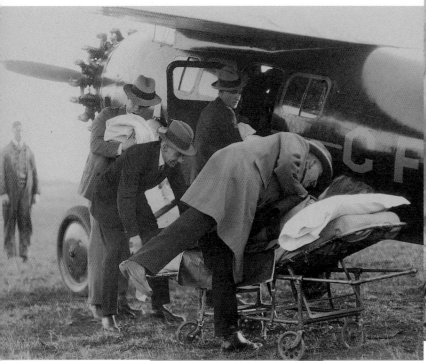

These women are members of the Salvation Army. The Salvation Army is a Christian organization that provides aid to victims of disasters around the world.

Air ambulances rush patients to the closest hospital.

These farmers are working together to build a barn.

What basic needs are being met in these historical photographs?

All people have basic needs. The physical needs for food, clothing, and shelter are one type of basic need. When people began to live in organized groups, they worked together to meet their physical needs. For example, one person could have been a fine bow-maker, and another person could have been a good spinner and weaver. These people could come together and cooperate. One could make a bow and quiver of arrows and exchange it for a warm woolen blanket. Or, all strong members of a group could cooperate by working together to build a home, a meeting place, or a bridge across a river.

As well as physical needs, humans have basic **psychological** needs. For example, people need to feel safe from harm. When groups cooperate, this need can be met by having trusted people responsible for safety and defense. Living in organized groups offers people protection and a way to defend their group.

When people live together, there are also basic **social** needs which must be satisfied. People need a common language for communication, for example. They need to share news and information. They also need to work together cooperatively and productively. To do this, a group needs rules, plans, and a way to make decisions.

A leader helps a group organize and make decisions. This is at the heart of the social need to have a form of government. Early groups of people discovered they needed at least one leader. A person became a leader by being the strongest, oldest, wisest, or most trustworthy. It was the leader's task to help the group organize in order to meet their basic needs.

The first forms of government began when early groups of people began to live together in groups of families. Through time, groups settled and formed villages. Eventually many of the villages developed into towns, and then into cities. Many of these settlements had kings, queens, or rich people as their leaders. The closer together people lived, the more they needed to work together to create a peaceful, safe community. Around the world and throughout history, groups of people have tried different ways of organizing to meet their needs.

As you read on, you will discover how three groups of people organized government. Each of these groups were very different. They lived in different parts of the world, and at different times in history. By examining different styles of government, you will see that people organized in different ways to meet their needs.

Vocabulary

ancestor –*n.* a grandparent, great-grandparent, or forebear

aristocracy –*n.* nobility, people who inherit highly-ranked positions in the community

corrupt –*adj.* a way of behaving that is dishonest or deceitful

debate –*v.* to discuss the arguments for and against an issue

democracy –*n.* a form of government that is elected and controlled by the people who live under it

descendant –*n.* child, grandchild, great-grandchild, and so on

despotism –*n.* dictatorship; one person or one party rule

direct democracy –*n.* a form of government in which people govern themselves, making the laws for their community together

dynasty –*n.* a series of rulers belonging to the same family

eligible –*adj.* being qualified, acceptable, able to be chosen

enfranchise –*v.* to give the right to participate

feudalism –*n.* a system of governing based on land use in exchange for service; feudalism existed from the 800s to 1400s in Europe

policies –*n.* plans of action

power –*n.* the authority to do a job or make a decision; the ability to control

psychological –*adj.* having to do with the mind

returning officer –*n.* the person who conducts an election locally and reports its results officially

right –*n.* something that is owed to a person by law, tradition, or nature

social –*adj.* having to do with being part of a community

virtuous –*adj.* a way of behaving that is valued

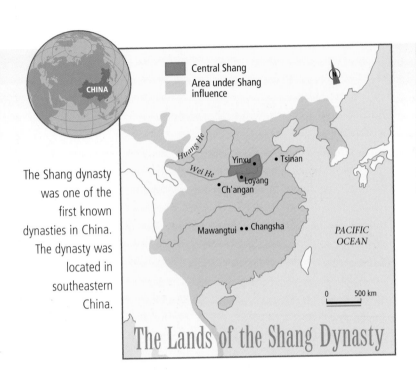

Central Shang
Area under Shang influence

CHINA

Huang He
Wei He
Yinxu • • Tsinan
• Loyang
• Ch'angan

Mawangtui •• Changsha

PACIFIC OCEAN

0   500 km

The Lands of the Shang Dynasty

The Shang dynasty was one of the first known dynasties in China. The dynasty was located in southeastern China.

This pitcher is a typical artifact from the era of the Shang dynasty.

Dynasties in Ancient China

Archaeologists tell us that there have been people living in China for more than half a million years. This is long before the beginning of written history. One of the first known forms of government in China was called a **dynasty.** For hundreds of years the dynasties ruled in China. The Shang dynasty is an example of one of the very first known Chinese dynasties.

The Shang dynasty began with a group of people who believed in a supreme god, Shang Ti. These ancient Chinese people believed that a **descendant** of their supreme god must be the king. When one king died, it would be his brother or his oldest son who would next become king.

This government was based on religious beliefs. The ancient Chinese believed that the first **ancestor** of an important family had the power to control the sun, moon, stars, rain, wind, and thunder. The first ancestor was a person who had died long before and was believed to live in an after-death spirit world. In the Shang dynasty, the first ancestor was Shang Ti. The people believed that their needs would be met if Shang Ti was pleased and honoured. This was done by making sacrifices to ensure the seasons would change, and by celebrations such as thanksgiving at harvest time. It was the responsibility of the king to lead the worship of his dead ancestor. The king was also believed to be able to communicate with Shang Ti.

Like other ancient civilizations, the Chinese built many communities near large rivers. The rivers helped the people meet their needs for food. Many early Chinese were farmers. The farmers worked the land for the king. They also served in the army to protect the king's land or to capture new lands.

The day-to-day work of the state was directed by the king. He was helped by members of

The agora was a busy place in ancient Greek city-states. Here, men attended meetings to discuss issues, and women shopped for food.

his family, but he held the power. One of the king's most important jobs was overseeing the control of floods and irrigation. It was also the king's responsibility to set taxes, make laws, and control the army.

Throughout history, and around the world, there are many examples of **despotism.** The dynasties of ancient China are one example of a form of government sometimes called despotism.

Your Turn

1. What do you think would be the advantages of one person having all the power?

2. What would be the disadvantages of one person having all the power?

3. Whose needs would be served best by this style of government?

City-States in Ancient Greece

Ancient Greece is known to have had large communities of people who grouped together to meet their basic needs. These communities were called city-states. At first these city-states were ruled by kings. Sometimes the king would ask the advice of wealthy nobles who lived in the city. The nobles, called the **aristocracy**, were usually the owners of the best land.

By 750 BCE, the nobles in most Greek city-states decided they did not need a king to make decisions. The nobles rebelled. For a while, the government was ruled by the nobles and a few very powerful people. During the 500s BCE, many people began to realize that they were just as important as the aristocracy. These people began to demand

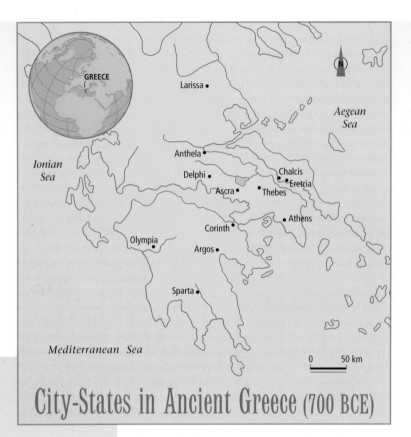

City-States in Ancient Greece (700 BCE)

The people of ancient Greece grouped together to form communities called city-states. This map shows the main city-states around 700 BCE.

Word Origins

Democracy comes from the ancient Greek word *demokratia; demos* meaning "people, free citizens" and *Kratos* meaning "power, rule, authority."

that they should also have a say in government. The idea of many people having a say in decision-making became more and more popular.

During the 400s BCE, Greek political thinkers like Plato and Aristotle encouraged the idea that there should be laws to guide how decisions were made. Athens became the first Greek city-state to change its government. It established a set of laws for the city-state. Special meetings or assemblies were held where citizens could discuss issues that affected their lives. It was the duty of every **eligible** male citizen living in Athens to take part in the assembly. At monthly meetings, laws were passed and **policies** were made. Members of the assembly also sat on juries to decide the innocence or guilt of those accused of breaking the laws. Women and slaves were not permitted to take part in meetings of the assembly.

In Athens, the assembly gathered at sunrise on a hill called the Pnyx. Sometimes there would be 4000 to 5000 men in attendance. They **debated** important issues and problems. The men would argue for hours and give their opinions on various issues and problems. One example of an issue might be whether or not to build a new temple to honour the Greek god Zeus. The men would have to weigh the arguments carefully in their minds. At the end of the debate, a vote was taken with a show of hands. Many people believe that these meetings, held more than 2000 years ago, were the beginnings of **democracy.**

This kind of government is called **direct democracy**. In a direct democracy, people govern themselves, making the laws for their community together. Everyone who is eligible to vote and who attends the meeting has the opportunity to have a say and vote on every decision.

Your Turn

1. What do you think would be the advantages of people sharing power?

2. What do you think would be the disadvantages of sharing power?

3. Whose needs would be served best by this style of government?

In feudal England, communities began growing around castles and manors. During the 1400s and 1500s, villages became centres for trade and government.

Feudalism in the Middle Ages in England

Beginning in the middle of the 400s CE, and lasting for nearly 600 years, many invaders tried to capture the lands of England. War, invasion, and bloodshed were part of normal life. Around the 600s to 700s CE, people began to organize under a military and political system called **feudalism.** During this period in history, there was no strong central government. Even a king only ruled over his own land. Communities grew around castles and manors built on clearings in the forests. The land was owned by powerful lords and farmed by peasants. Lords would give some of their land to less wealthy nobles who were called vassals. In turn, the lord expected the vassals to fight for him when he called them.

In the feudal system, vassals farmed a part of the lord's land. They kept part of the harvest for themselves and gave part of the harvest to the lord. When the vassal died, the land was then used by his son who had the same arrangement with the lord.

Disagreements among the vassals were settled in the lord's court. The lord acted as a judge. Sometimes, the feuding vassals were

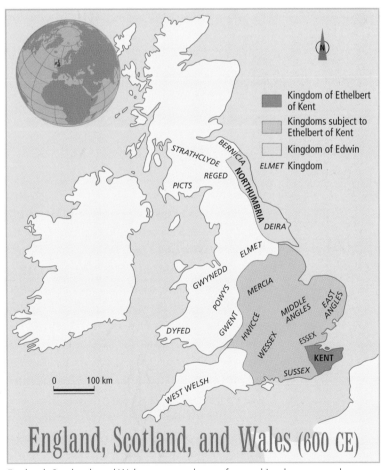

Kingdom of Ethelbert of Kent

Kingdoms subject to Ethelbert of Kent

Kingdom of Edwin

ELMET Kingdom

STRATHCLYDE
BERNICIA
REGED
NORTHUMBRIA
PICTS
DEIRA
ELMET
GWYNEDD
POWYS
MERCIA
GWENT
HWICCE
MIDDLE ANGLES
EAST ANGLES
DYFED
WESSEX
ESSEX
KENT
SUSSEX
WEST WELSH

0   100 km

England, Scotland, and Wales (600 CE)

England, Scotland, and Wales were made up of many kingdoms around 600 CE. During these feudal times, there was no strong central government. Whoever owned land was the ruler of it.

required to solve their problem in a "trial by combat." This involved a fight, after which the victor was declared the winner of the case. Often, disagreements were heard in the lord's court and the final judgement was made by the other vassals.

Feudalism lasted more than 500 years. As villages and then cities grew larger, there was a need for greater organization. Across the land, government that would meet the changing needs of the people began to form.

Your Turn

1. What do you think would be the advantages of a few people having all the power?

2. What do you think would be the disadvantages of a few people having all the power?

3. Whose needs would be served best by this style of government?

For Whom Does Government Work?

Aristotle was a well-known thinker in ancient Greece. He was especially interested in thinking about how governments worked. Aristotle believed that some forms of government work for the common good. He called these governments **virtuous.** Aristotle also believed some forms of government work to make life better only for the leaders. He called these governments **corrupt.**

Aristotle thought that it would be best to have one or a few virtuous leaders, but he also knew it was difficult to find them. He concluded that the best form of government for most people, most of the time, would be a democracy. In a democracy, the people could hold the rulers in check and keep them from becoming corrupt.

Aristotle was a philosopher who lived from 384 to 322 BCE in ancient Greece. His book called *Politics* described how he thought government should be organized.

Your Turn

1. How do you think Aristotle would classify the dynasties of ancient China, the direct democracy system in ancient Greece, and the feudal system in England?

2. How would you classify the leadership of your school or classroom?

3. If you were to design a government, which form would you choose? Why?

The chart on the opposite page shows the way Aristotle classified forms of governments. Aristotle looked at government in many different ways, but he lived at a time when women in Greece did not have a voice in government. We cannot tell, by looking at the chart, what he thought about women having a voice.

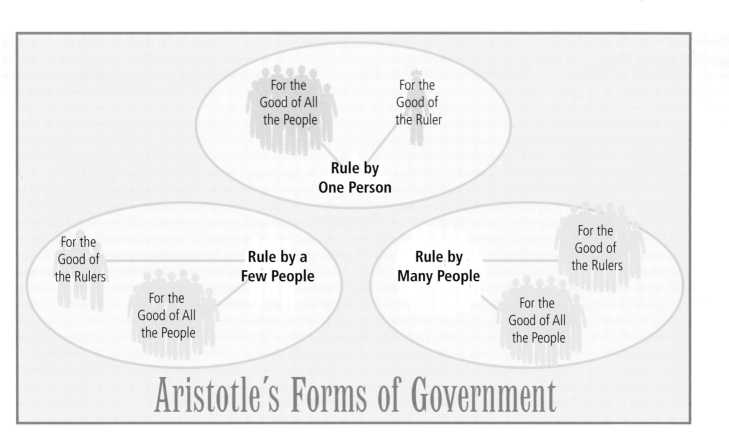

Aristotle's Forms of Government

Rule by
One Person

For the
Good of All
the People

For the
Good of
the Ruler

Rule by a
Few People

For the
Good of
the Rulers

For the
Good of All
the People

Rule by
Many People

For the
Good of
the Rulers

For the
Good of All
the People

Your Turn

1. If you had the opportunity to talk to Aristotle about women having a voice in government decision-making, what would you say?

2. Do you think Aristotle's description of governments would need to change to include women? Why?

3. As you go on to learn about government in Canada, try to decide where it would fit on Aristotle's chart.

Power:
Where Does It Come From?

When people are given an opportunity to speak up, they have the power to influence other people. One way this happens is through discussion or debate of issues. The **right** to vote on a decision also gives a person power. Being directly involved makes a person feel respected. It also makes a person feel like he or she belongs to the group. When a person feels he or she has been a part of a decision, often he or she is more likely to help make the decision work.

Your Turn

In ancient Greece, only some men had the powers of voice and the right to vote. Women and slaves were not **enfranchised.**

1. When have you ever thought that your opinion did not count?

2. Have you ever been told a decision is not yours to make? How did you feel?

Women's Right to Vote

This profile examines one group of people who were told they could not have a voice in choosing leaders. For most of European history, only men were allowed to vote. Women did not have a voice. This tradition continued when Europeans settled in Canada. As you read this profile, discover how women organized to change the rules about who could vote in government elections.

In the late 1800s, women in many countries of the world began to organize. They wanted change. Women wanted equal rights to education, equal wages for equal work, and the opportunity to vote. Canada was one of the countries where women were unhappy that only men were allowed to make decisions for the people. Women who worked to change the laws to allow women to vote were called suffragists.

Nellie McClung was one Canadian suffragist. As a young woman, Nellie lived in the province of Manitoba. She objected to the differences in men's and women's rights. Nellie joined a group called the Winnipeg Political Equality League. This group was committed to changing the law so that women could vote.

Until that time, many men were convinced that giving the vote to women would be disastrous. Many speeches were made by men objecting to granting the vote to women.

Nellie's group decided to try something different. They staged a play at a Winnipeg theatre. It was a play that made fun of some of the men's speeches about why women should not vote. Nellie used a speech that had been given by a man. Wherever the speech used the word "women," Nellie changed it to "men." In the play she said:

"The trouble is that if men start to vote, they will vote too much. Politics unsettles men, and unsettled

Nellie McClung lived from 1873 to 1951. She believed that women should have the same political rights as men.

men means unsettled bills, broken furniture, broken vows, and divorce ... If men were to get into the habit of voting, who knows what might happen — it's hard enough to keep them at home now."

Nellie's part in the play was especially funny. People laughed at how silly the argument sounded. Most people could see the problem with the men's position. Try reading the speech using the word women instead of men. Can you see a problem with the argument?

In 1914, Nellie moved to Alberta with her husband. She carried on her work as a suffragist. Nellie's work and that of other suffragists was successful in 1916 when women in Alberta, Saskatchewan, and Manitoba won the right to vote. It was the middle of the century when all women finally gained the right to vote in all parts of Canada.

Ideas for Gathering Information:
Locating World History

This chapter has been an introduction to some governments in history. To learn more about governments, you may want to visit the library. The library is an excellent community service with a variety of resources and research tools. Research tools such as online catalogues and Internet web search engines can help you locate information.

Resources are materials which contain information. When you want to gather historical information, the following resources are useful:

➤ encyclopedias
➤ CD-ROMs
➤ Internet
➤ books
➤ videos
➤ newspapers and magazines

Historical information can be found in reference resources like encyclopedias. Encyclopedias have a subject index that may be located in one volume or at the end of the last volume in the series. Many encyclopedias are found on CD-ROM. CD-ROMs have search tools for you to use.

Encyclopedias are also a good starting place if you are curious about other styles of government. If you want to learn about the government in a specific country, begin by looking up the name of the country. Some styles of government are associated with a culture rather than a country. Examples of this would be found if you researched cultures like the Aztec, Inca, or Maya. If you already know the name of a specific style of government, such as despotism, you can begin your search with that term. You can use these key words to search for information on the Internet, too.

Historical information can also be found in the nonfiction books section of the library. Because our understanding of history can change when new information is uncovered, it is important to look for the most current publications on the subject you are researching. (You will find the date of publication in the first few pages of the book.) It is always a good idea to check two or three resources to see if the information agrees. You will also find history on educational videos, and in journals and magazines that are specifically published to preserve culture and heritage.

When you are examining historical information you must be a critical thinker. This means you must evaluate the information you find. The following questions will help you to evaluate.

➤ Is this factual information or is it opinion?

➤ Is the information accurate? What other sources say the same thing?

➤ Do you think the information has been presented fairly? Should you look for other opinions?

➤ What kind of facts support the information?

➤ From whose point of view has the information been presented?

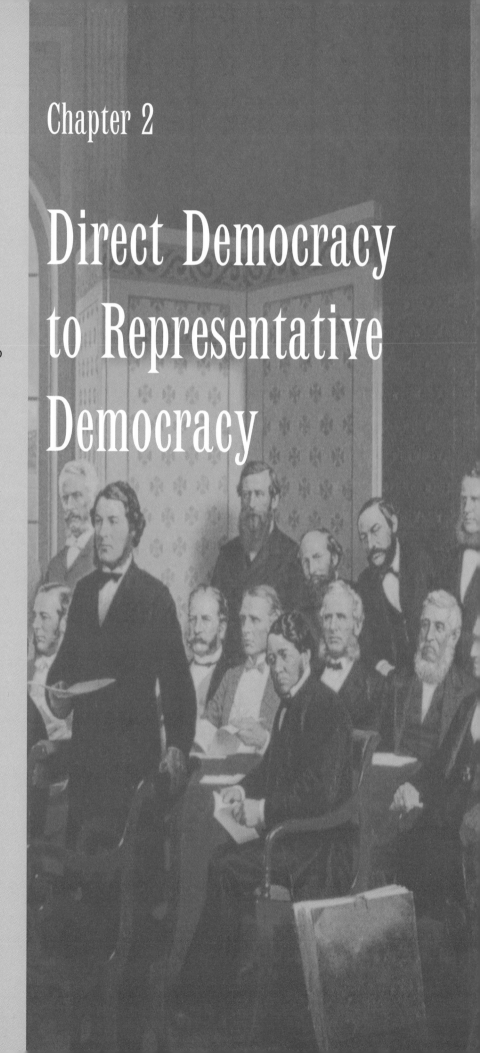

Chapter Focus

Many people want to have a voice in decision-making. The system used by the ancient Greeks, however, would not be practical in a country where a large population is spread out over great distances. **Representative democracy,** Canada's system of government today, enables people to communicate their needs and opinions to **elected** representatives.

In this chapter, you will be introduced to one of the earliest forms of government in Canada. You will see how Canadians organized to create a plan for **responsible** and representative government. You will also examine the advantages and disadvantages of representative democracy.

As you read this chapter, consider these questions:

➤ What kind of government did Native peoples use?

➤ How was a government formed for Canada?

➤ Why did Canada need responsible government?

➤ Why choose representative government?

Chapter 2

Direct Democracy to Representative Democracy

Vocabulary

archive –*n.* a library or storehouse for historical information

colony –*n.* a settlement of people in a new land some distance from their home community

Confederation –*n.* an official joining together of governments

constitution –*n.* the rules and beliefs which guide the work of government

council –*n.* a group or special committee that gives advice

Dominion –*n.* a self-governing nation within the British Commonwealth

elected –*adj.* a person chosen in a vote

ensure –*v.* to guarantee or make something happen

federal –*adj.* a form of government; the central government in Canada

federation –*n.* a league or union of groups

House of Commons –*n.* the elected Members of Parliament in the federal government

loyal –*adj.* being dependable and faithful

maritime –*adj.* located by the sea

parliament –*n.* assembly of representatives; a legislative (lawmaking) body; Canada's Parliament today is the federal lawmaking body consisting of the House of Commons (elected) and the Senate (appointed)

plebiscite –*n.* a vote taken on an issue among all citizens

representative democracy –*n.* a style of government in which voters elect people to speak on their behalf

representatives –*n.* those chosen to act or speak for others

responsible –*adj.* answerable to the people or their representatives

returning officer –*n.* the person who conducts an election locally and reports its results officially

riding –*n.* a district (area) represented by members of a lawmaking body; a constituency

township –*n.* a unit of government in central Canada; a survey unit of land on Canada's prairies

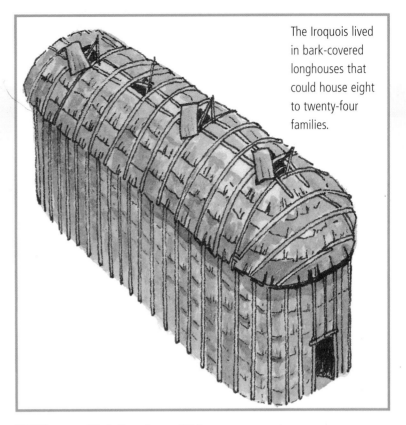

The Iroquois lived in bark-covered longhouses that could house eight to twenty-four families.

What Did the First Governments Look Like in This Land?

Throughout the lands that would later be called Canada, people had been living in communities for many thousands of years. These were the Native peoples. All Native communities had a form of government.

There were many ways the people governed themselves. The Salish on the west coast, for example, were very different from the Inuit on the north coast and from the Mi'Kmaq on the east coast. Some Native peoples moved according to the migrations of animals which they hunted. Others lived in villages, growing crops and hunting. Because the people met their needs in different ways, they governed themselves differently, too.

The Iroquois

One example of an early Native government is the Iroquois. Iroquois nations inhabited lands which later became parts of eastern

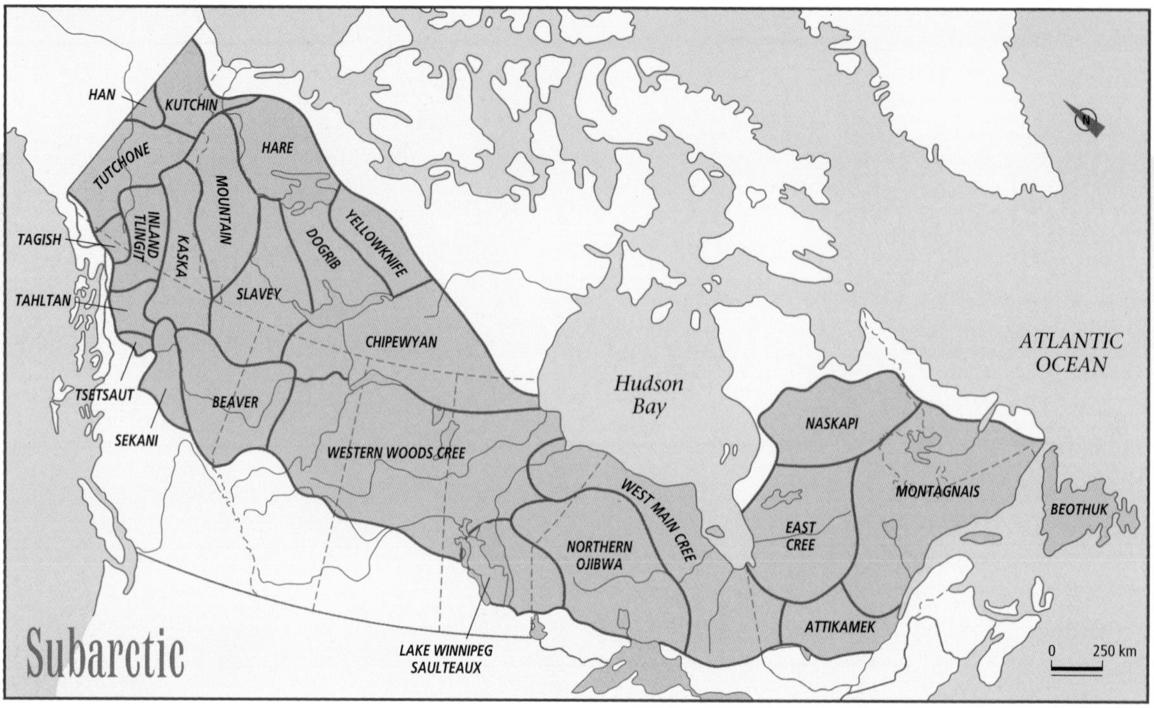
HAN
KUTCHIN
TUTCHONE
HARE
INLAND TLINGIT
MOUNTAIN
YELLOWKNIFE
TAGISH
KASKA
DOGRIB
TAHLTAN
SLAVEY
CHIPEWYAN
TSETSAUT
BEAVER
SEKANI
WESTERN WOODS CREE
Hudson Bay
ATLANTIC OCEAN
NASKAPI
MONTAGNAIS
BEOTHUK
WEST MAIN CREE
EAST CREE
NORTHERN OJIBWA
ATTIKAMEK
LAKE WINNIPEG SAULTEAUX
0 250 km
N
Subarctic

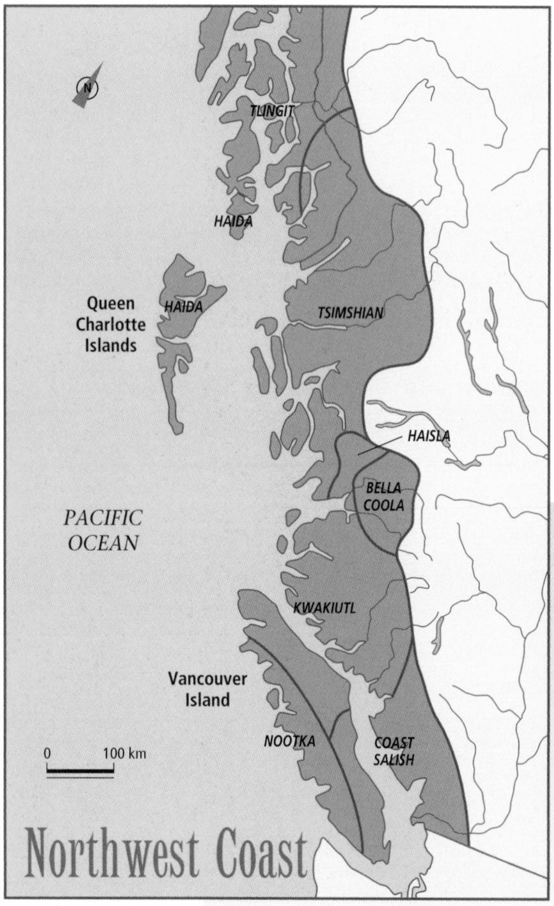
N
TLINGIT
HAIDA
Queen Charlotte Islands
HAIDA
TSIMSHIAN
HAISLA
BELLA COOLA
PACIFIC OCEAN
KWAKIUTL
Vancouver Island
0 100 km
NOOTKA
COAST SALISH
Northwest Coast

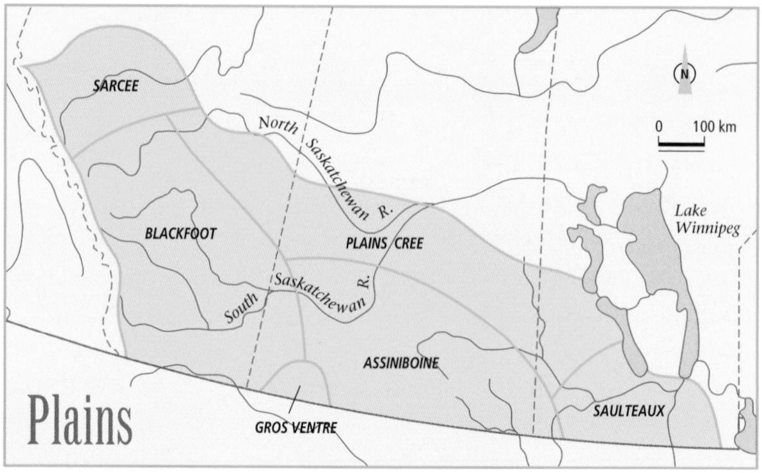
SARCEE
N
0 100 km
North Saskatchewan R.
Lake Winnipeg
BLACKFOOT
PLAINS CREE
South Saskatchewan R.
ASSINIBOINE
GROS VENTRE
SAULTEAUX
Plains

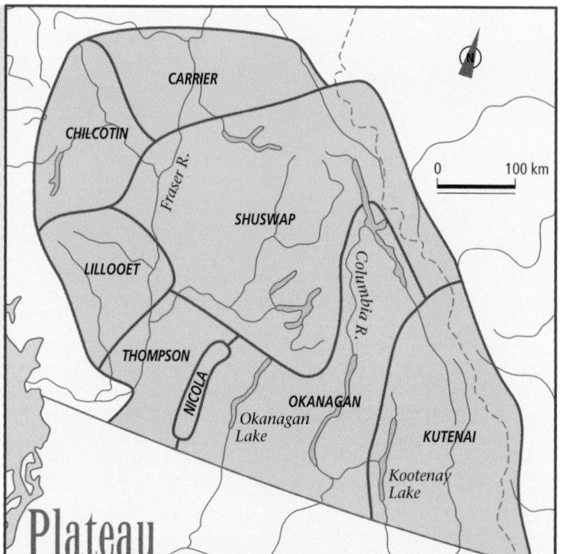
N
CARRIER
CHILCOTIN
0 100 km
Fraser R.
SHUSWAP
LILLOOET
Columbia R.
THOMPSON
NICOLA
OKANAGAN
Okanagan Lake
KUTENAI
Kootenay Lake
Plateau

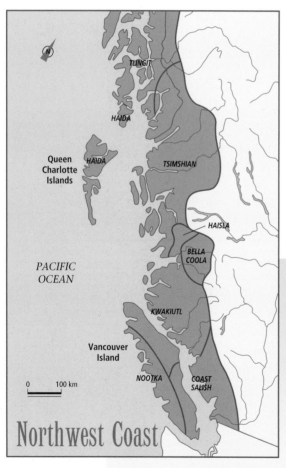

Traditional Lands of the Native Peoples

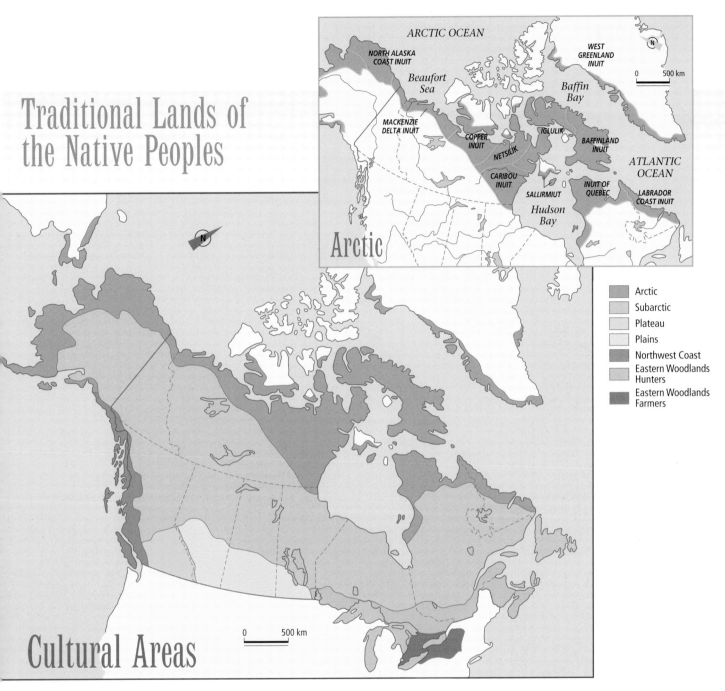

Arctic

- Arctic
- Subarctic
- Plateau
- Plains
- Northwest Coast
- Eastern Woodlands Hunters
- Eastern Woodlands Farmers

ARCTIC OCEAN

NORTH ALASKA COAST INUIT

WEST GREENLAND INUIT

Beaufort Sea

Baffin Bay

MACKENZIE DELTA INUIT

COPPER INUIT

IGLULIK

NETSILIK

BAFFINLAND INUIT

ATLANTIC OCEAN

CARIBOU INUIT

SALLIRMIUT

INUIT OF QUEBEC

LABRADOR COAST INUIT

Hudson Bay

Cultural Areas

0   500 km

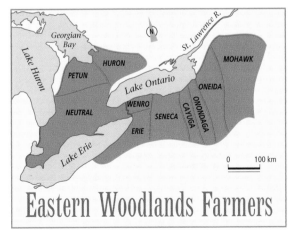

Eastern Woodlands Farmers

Georgian Bay

Lake Huron

HURON

PETUN

St. Lawrence R.

MOHAWK

Lake Ontario

ONEIDA

NEUTRAL

WENRO

SENECA

CAYUGA

ONONDAGA

ERIE

Lake Erie

0   100 km

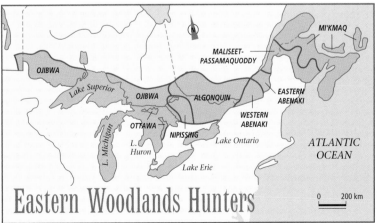

Eastern Woodlands Hunters

MI'KMAQ

OJIBWA

MALISEET-PASSAMAQUODDY

Lake Superior

OJIBWA

ALGONQUIN

EASTERN ABENAKI

L. Michigan

OTTAWA

NIPISSING

WESTERN ABENAKI

L. Huron

Lake Ontario

ATLANTIC OCEAN

Lake Erie

0   200 km

Canada and the United States. The Iroquois called themselves *Ongwanonhsioni,* which means "we longhouse builders." This name described their homes, which were bark-covered buildings 20 metres long and 6 metres wide. Inside, longhouses were divided into apartments which housed eight to twenty-four families.

There were several nations of Iroquois. Around 1400 CE, five nations joined together into a larger group called a **federation.** These nations were the Mohawk, the Oneida, the Onondaga, the Seneca, and the Cayuga. Historians believe that Hiawatha, a great Mohawk chief, formed the federation to keep peace among the nations. Hiawatha asked each nation to send a number of leaders to a meeting. These leaders were called *sachem.* Sachem means elder, guide, advisor, counsellor, or teacher. The sachem were chosen by women.

Women were held in high esteem by the people. This is why they had the important job of choosing sachem. Like Mother Earth, women were seen as givers of life and were valued providers for the family. An older woman ruled each family or clan. She lived in the apartment nearest to the door of the longhouse. It was the ruling woman who spoke with the other women in the family when it was time to name a new sachem.

Together, the sachem formed the great federation **council**, which became known as the League of Five Nations. (This federation council could be compared to the **federal** government in Canada today.) About 300 years later another Iroquois nation, the Tuscarora, joined the federation. The federation then became known as the Six Nations.

How Was Government Organized for British and French Settlers?

After the formation of the Iroquois federation, British and French settlement began in North America. In 1497, John Cabot reached what later became known as Newfoundland. He claimed the land for Britain. In 1534, Jacques Cartier explored the Gulf of the St. Lawrence River. He claimed the land for France. In 1604 Samuel de Champlain founded Port Royal, the first French settlement in the **colony** of Acadia. (Today we know Acadia as Nova Scotia, Prince Edward Island, and New Brunswick.)

South of the French colony of Acadia, the British had established the New England colonies. (The New England colonies are now part of the United States.) In 1608 Champlain built a fort at Quebec, around which the colony of New France grew. (The fort at Quebec later became present-day Quebec City.)

There was little peace between the colonies of Britain and France. The two countries were enemies in Europe, and battles were fought in North America, too. Each country fought to take over the other's colonies.

Your Turn

1. Some people would say Hiawatha was thinking of the "greater good" when he brought the nations together. What do you think this expression means?

2. In Canada today, we organize ourselves into large communities such as villages, towns, and cities. These communities are within areas called provinces or territories. In turn, the provinces and territories are part of a larger organization called Canada.

   What similarities can you see between the early government of the Iroquois and the way government in Canada is organized today?

3. As you learn more about different forms of government, compare them to the early government of the Iroquois. What is similar? What is different?

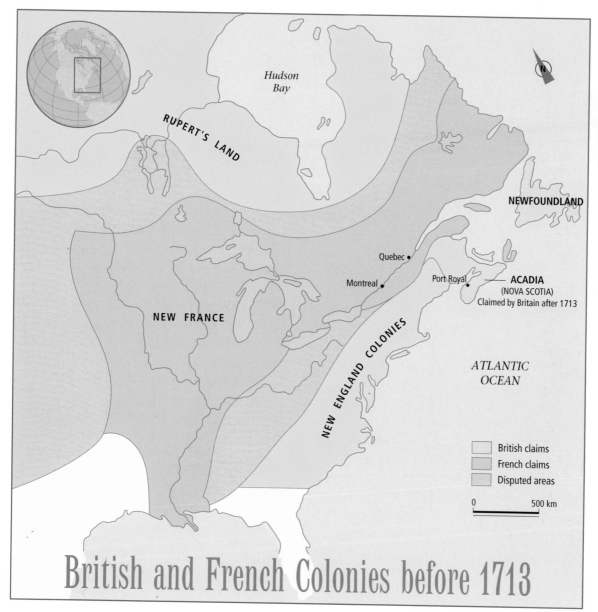

Which colonies belonged to France before 1713? To the British?

British and French Colonies before 1713

Direct government was not possible for the French and British who settled in the colonies. The kings and queens of France and Britain lived across the Atlantic Ocean. Many decisions needed to be made quickly but the journey by ship took from three to seven weeks. So, the kings and queens chose trusted people to govern as their **representatives.** These representatives made decisions they believed their queens or kings would want. They acted to **ensure** that the interests of the kings or queens were met.

For 100 years, Britain and France battled for control of the colonies. In 1713, Britain won control of Acadia from France. Then in 1759, the French and British battled on the Plains of Abraham, just outside the walls of the French settlement at Quebec. They were fighting for control of New France. In just 10 minutes, the battle was over. Britain had claimed the right to control the colony of New France.

Your Turn

1. How do you think the French would have felt about living under British rule?

2. What do you think might cause the French concern?

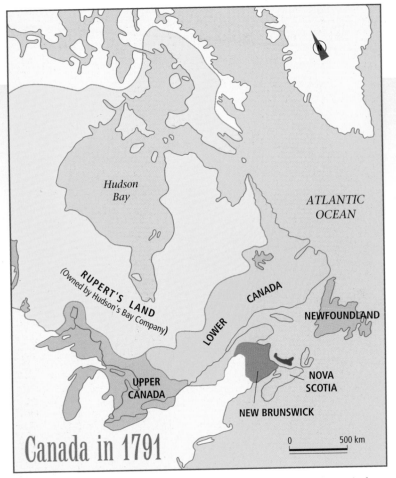

Canada in 1791

Compare this map of Canada to the map of British and French colonies before 1713. Describe the changes that have occurred.

Representative Government and Responsible Government

By 1791, the system of government in Canada included two elected assemblies. One assembly was for Upper Canada. The other was for Lower Canada. Britain's appointed representatives controlled the decision-making. Both Upper and Lower Canada each had a lieutenant-governor who was appointed by Britain. The lieutenant-governor appointed a legislative council and an executive council. This system of government was called representative government.

Many people in the colonies were unhappy with the power of the appointed representatives. These representatives were responsible to the king of Britain, but not to the people. By the middle 1800s, many colonists felt that decisions about the Canadas should be made by the people who lived in the colonies. The

In 1791, there were two elected assemblies in Canada. One was for Upper Canada, and the other was for Lower Canada. (Today, Upper Canada is known as the province of Ontario. Lower Canada is known as the province of Quebec.)

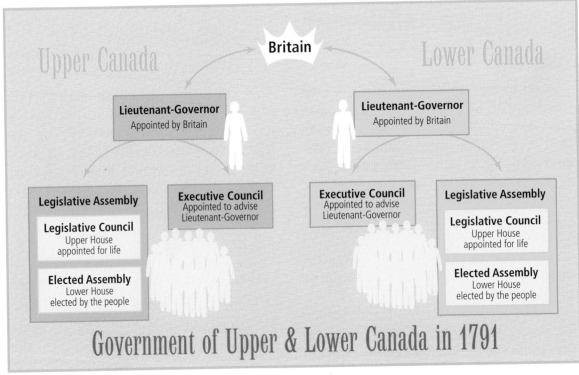

Government of Upper & Lower Canada in 1791

colonists rebelled against their government. They wanted a government in which the representatives they elected would have a greater voice.

The British government appointed Lord Durham as governor general of British North America. His task was to investigate the situation and make recommendations for the future government of the colonies. Lord Durham made a number of important recommendations. He recommended that Upper and Lower Canada be joined as the Province of Canada, and that it have one elected assembly. Each of the Canadas would elect 42 members to the new assembly. These elected representatives of the assembly would have most of the power. The council of representatives appointed by the British government was responsible for taking the advice of elected representatives, rather than the other way around. Lord Durham's recommendations described responsible government, in which elected representatives have control of lawmaking.

Lord Durham recommended that Upper and Lower Canada be joined as the Province of Canada, and that it have one elected assembly.

Your Turn

1. What do you see as the differences between representative and responsible government?

2. Why do you think responsible government was so important to Canada?

3. Who had the power in responsible government? Why?

Achieving Confederation

Lord Durham's recommendations resulted in many changes. Among them were new names for the colonies. Upper Canada was renamed Canada West. Lower Canada was renamed Canada East. Together, they were called the Province of Canada. Other important changes occurred to improve the way the government served the people. Organization of the assembly, however, was a problem. There were disagreements between the elected representatives from Canada East and Canada West. Each colony had the same number of elected representatives. This often resulted in tied votes.

The Fathers of Confederation were the 33 representatives from the Province of Canada and the maritime colonies (except Prince Edward Island) who wrote a constitution for the Dominion of Canada. John A. Macdonald (the person standing in front of the middle window) became the first prime minister.

In 1864, a group of representatives from the Province of Canada and the **maritime** colonies (Prince Edward Island, Nova Scotia, and New Brunswick) met to discuss better ways of governing. They had the idea that by forming one government for all these colonies, they could create a great country. After 17 days of discussion, they had written a **constitution.** This constitution stated that people in the colonies should remain **loyal** to Britain. It stated that the colonies should be organized as provinces under a general government. Today we call that general government our federal government.

The constitutional plan also described how each province would send elected representatives to a central **parliament.** Parliament would have responsibility for making laws for all parts of the country. This new government would be a **parliamentary democracy.**

By the time the meetings ended, the constitution listed the responsibilities of the federal and provincial governments. Also, an agreement had been made to construct a railway linking the Province of Canada with the maritime colonies.

Before **Confederation** could take place, the constitution had to be approved by the people living in all of the colonies, as well as the British parliament. In 1867, Queen Victoria of Britain signed the British North America Act. This act made the constitutional plan of the colonists a reality. The colonies became the **Dominion** of Canada on July 1, 1867. Sir John A. Macdonald, one of the representatives, became the first prime minister of Canada. Along with the other 32 representatives, he is also remembered as one of the Fathers of Confederation.

How Did the Government Work After Confederation?

The new country was made up of four provinces: Ontario, Quebec, Nova Scotia, and New Brunswick. (Prince Edward Island decided to wait another six years before joining Confederation.) Each province elected representatives to the **House of Commons** in the new federal government. These representatives were responsible to the people of Canada rather than to a ruler in Britain. This meant that Canada had become a representative democracy.

Representative democracy works the same way in a country, a province, a city, or a town.

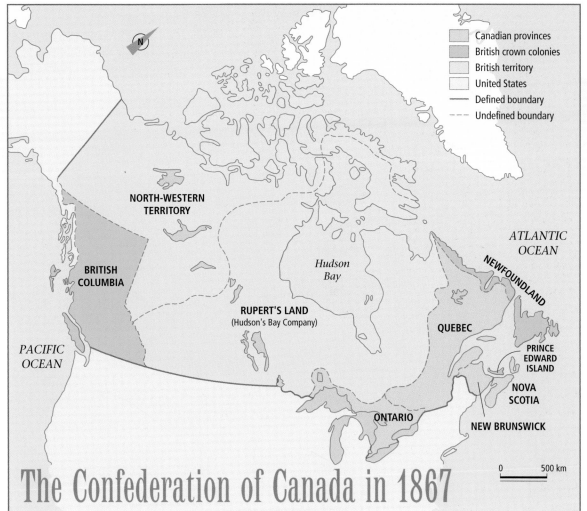

The Confederation of Canada in 1867

Canadian provinces
British crown colonies
British territory
United States
— Defined boundary
- - - Undefined boundary

In 1867, the Dominion of Canada consisted of Ontario, Quebec, Nova Scotia, and New Brunswick.

Today, there are many representative democracies across Canada. With every form of government there are advantages and disadvantages. When examining a form of government, it is important to examine these advantages and disadvantages.

Some Advantages of Representative Democracy in Canada

➤ practical when people are spread over a large area

➤ majority of citizens can spend time working in other ways

➤ becomes possible to pay a small number of elected representatives to work full time at making informed decisions

Some Disadvantages of Representative Democracy in Canada

➤ people have less say in decisions that affect them

➤ some people do not believe that they can make a difference; so, they give up their responsibility for being informed

Your Turn

1. Can you think of other advantages that could be listed here?

2. Can you think of other disadvantages that could be listed here?

The Dominion of Canada in 1873

Map legend:
- Canadian provinces
- Canadian territories
- British territories
- United States
- Defined boundary
- Undefined boundary

Map labels: NORTHWEST TERRITORIES, BRITISH COLUMBIA, Hudson Bay, ATLANTIC OCEAN, NEWFOUNDLAND, PACIFIC OCEAN, MANITOBA, QUEBEC, PRINCE EDWARD ISLAND, NOVA SCOTIA, ONTARIO, NEW BRUNSWICK, 0 500 km

Dates that the Provinces and Territories Joined Confederation

Ontario	1867
Quebec	1867
New Brunswick	1867
Nova Scotia	1867
Manitoba	1870
Northwest Territories	1870
British Columbia	1871
Prince Edward Island	1873
Yukon	1898
Alberta	1905
Saskatchewan	1905
Newfoundland	1949
Nunavut	1999

More Governments Since 1867

The map of Canada has changed several times since July 1, 1867. In 1870, three years after Confederation, the Canadian government bought a vast amount of land from the Hudson's Bay Company. This land, 20 234 hectares around the company's trading posts, plus 3773 hectares in every **township**, was known as the Northwest Territories.

As more settlers arrived in Ontario and Quebec, more land from the Northwest Territories was added to these provinces. Other parts of the Northwest Territories became the provinces of Manitoba, Alberta, and Saskatchewan. The federal government took responsibility for governing the remaining Northwest Territories.

In the late 1800s, gold was discovered on the banks of Rabbit Creek (later called Bonanza Creek) in the Northwest Territories. Thousands of miners and settlers rushed to the Northwest Territories from Europe, southern Canada, and the United States to claim land with gold in it. With this sudden population growth, the federal government decided to divide the Northwest Territories again. The lands of the gold rush became the Yukon Territory.

The federal government created the Yukon Territorial Government in 1898. The territorial government consisted of a commissioner appointed by the federal government and a council of citizens of Yukon Territory. The job of the commissioner was to work for both the federal government and for the territorial government.

When the gold rush ended, the population of Canada's North was considered too small and spread out to form provincial governments. Today, both the Yukon Territory and the Northwest Territories continue to have territorial governments. Although territorial governments do not have as many powers as provincial governments, they continue to have an elected council of people who live in the territories. In 1999, a new territory will be formed called Nunavut.

Profile:
A New Government in Canada

In April 1999, Canada will have a new territory called Nunavut. The territory will be home to about 25 000 people, more than 17 000 of whom will be Inuit. Nunavut is being formed because the people of the eastern Arctic feel that the Northwest Territories is so large that it is difficult for the territorial government in faraway Yellowknife to meet their needs.

For many years, there were meetings among the federal government, the people of the eastern Arctic, and the people of the western Arctic. They discussed how a new government would work, and how government responsibilities would be divided. They talked about how resources would be looked after and how the people in the western Arctic would be affected. They decided where the new line on the map of Canada would be drawn. Finally, they decided that 2 000 000 square kilometres of the Northwest Territories will become Nunavut. This area of land is almost twice the size of the province of British Columbia.

Forming a new government takes money. The federal government has set aside $150 million to help establish the new territory. Some of the money will help construct new buildings, set up offices, and pay government employees.

Forming a new government also takes careful planning. Representatives from the federal government, Yukon and Northwest Territories governments, and the eastern Arctic are working to make a plan for success.

In 1999, Nunavut will be formed from a large part of the Northwest Territories. The majority of the people in this new territory will be Inuit. The name Nunavut means "Our Land."

The capital city of Nunavut will be Iqaluit, a community of 4000 people located on Baffin Island. The Nunavut planning committee considered allowing each **riding** to elect two representatives to the territorial government. One representative would be female, and the other would be male. In the rest of Canada, each riding elects only one representative to provincial or territorial government. In May 1997, however, a special vote called a **plebiscite** showed that most of the people of the eastern Arctic were against having both a female and a male representative.

Your Turn

1. What reasons do you think the Nunavut planners had for recommending that each riding have a female and a male representative?

2. Why do you think the people of the eastern Arctic voted "no" to this plan?

Ideas for Gathering Information:
Searching for Local History

Most communities keep records of the history of their local government. There are many interesting stories to be found in these old materials.

Two main sources can help you search for such stories. One source is in your public library. Check the card or online catalogue. Another source is an **archive**, a special type of library for historical information. Archives are sometimes kept in your local government building. If you have a museum in your community, the archive might be there.

Before you begin a search, it is best to write a description of what kind of information you are looking for and how you plan to use the information. This will help an archivist identify materials that will be most helpful to you. In most cases, you cannot take materials out of an archive because they cannot be replaced if they are lost. It is important that you have clean hands and handle the old materials gently. Make sure to give yourself plenty of time.

Some of the most interesting stories come from local historians. Many local historians have recorded their memories in books. These books can often be found at local libraries. You may also be fortunate enough to be able to talk with a local historian. If this is the case, prepare a few guiding questions before the interview. Be sure you tell the historian what kind of

Early settlers wanted schools so that their children could have an education. School boards became the earliest form of local government in many areas.

An Edmonton Story

In 1884 a hot election took place on a cold winter day in Edmonton. This was during the time when schools were paid for by people who thought education was important. They were mostly people who had children. The people thought that if they could establish a school board, the schools could be paid for by taxes. The people decided to hold a vote.

The parents were enthusiastic about this plan, but single men and business people were not. They didn't like the idea of paying taxes for a service that they thought would be useless to them. The Hudson's Bay Company was one business that did not want to pay a school tax. As voting day drew near, the employees came up with a plan. The Hudson's Bay Company arranged for their employees to travel to Edmonton from their posts at Calgary, Slave Lake, and Athabaska Landing. They were asked to vote against setting up a school board.

In the meantime, the people who wanted the school board were wondering what they could do to make sure their side won the vote. Donald Ross was the owner of the Edmonton Hotel. He made it his business to ask all the guests staying at his hotel to vote in favour of setting up a school board.

On voting day, the temperature dropped far below zero degrees Celsius. The Hudson's Bay Company employees voted. The parents voted. Mr. Ross again asked his guests to get out and vote. The day was so cold, they told him, that they didn't want to go outside. Among them all, there was only one raccoon coat that would keep a person warm on such a day. Mr. Ross told them to take turns wearing the coat and he drove them in his sleigh, one by one, to the voting hall.

The **returning officer** quickly learned that another "yes" vote was entering the hall when he saw the raccoon coat in the doorway again! In the end, the vote was in favour of establishing the school board. Edmonton was on the way to forming a first local government.

information you are seeking. Many people find it helpful to tape record the interviews. Be sure to ask permission to use a tape recorder when you arrange the interview.

The above is an example of a story from Edmonton, Alberta's local history.

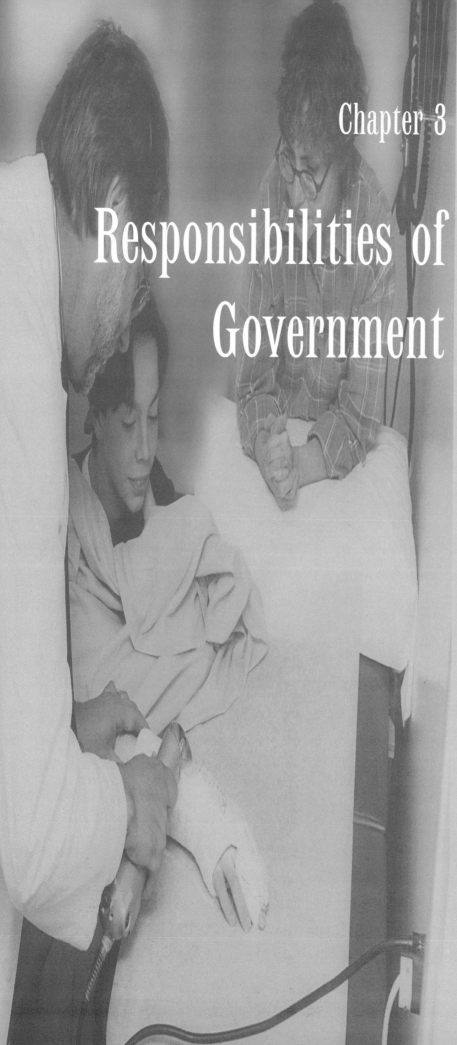

Responsibilities of Government

Government in Canada has the responsibility of helping Canadians meet needs that cannot be easily met by families, individuals, or by businesses. In modern times, people depend on government to help meet physical, social, and psychological needs.

In Canada, a person who works in a bank may count on a farmer to grow the vegetables that will feed her family. In turn, the farmer may depend on a trucker to move the vegetables to the banker's community. Truckers may depend on being able to travel on safe, well-constructed roads. When people work together in this way, we say they are **interdependent.**

Our governments help us work interdependently. It is the responsibility of governments, for example, to establish rules for which chemicals can be sprayed on the farmer's crops and what quality of food can be sold in our stores. Rules for where large trucks can travel and the design, construction, and care of our roads are all part of the responsibilities of government.

Canadian government is organized in three levels. These levels are the federal government, provincial or territorial government, and local government.

As you read this chapter, consider these questions:

➤ What are the responsibilities of government?

➤ How do laws help the people?

➤ How does the federal government ensure that people are fairly represented?

➤ What is the role of an elected representative?

➤ What are **minority** rights?

How Are Your Needs Being Met?

Habitat for Humanity helps to build homes for people who cannot afford to do so.

In previous chapters, you have seen that people in a **society** have many basic needs. These needs are physical, social, and psychological.

In a community, a province or territory, and in a country, there are needs shared by people living in the group. For example, when people in a community worship together, they are meeting a psychological need.

The Food Bank collects food donations from people and companies and gives them to people who cannot afford to buy groceries.

When people in a community support a newspaper, they are meeting a social need. When neighbours share food with each other, they are meeting a physical need.

When members of a community are experiencing difficulty meeting basic needs, communities work cooperatively to help. They have governments that organize services such as hospitals and schools. Volunteering is one

Vocabulary

by-law −*n.* a law made by a local government

census −*n.* an official count of the people in the community

constituency −*n.* a district (area) represented by members of a lawmaking body; a riding

discriminated against −*v.* isolated, treated unfairly

gender −*n.* sex; male or female

integrity −*n.* honesty, self respect

interdependent −*adj.* dependent or reliant on one another

interpret −*v.* to explain or translate; to apply (a law)

majority −*n.* more than half; those who are in the greater number

minority −*n.* less than half; those who are out-numbered

society −*n.* an organized human grouping, community

subsidize −*v.* to assist, or to support with money

Finding Your Voice

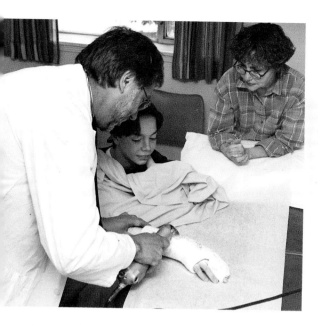

Many people rely on social assistance to pay the expense of medical care.

other special way community members help each other meet their needs.

People who are unable to meet their needs can ask for help from government. This help, called social assistance, provides money and **subsidized** services for people. Social assistance is a way Canadians have organized to try to ensure that people have the food, clothing, shelter, and medical care they need to survive.

Your Turn

1. Do you have a Food Bank, a Salvation Army Thrift Store, or a Habitat for Humanity office in your community?

2. How do these organizations help people meet their needs?

3. Who runs these organizations?

4. List the ways people in your community organize to help others meet their needs.

5. Make a list of your needs. Decide whether each need would be best met by your family, community volunteers, by business, or by government. Give reasons for your decisions.

What Needs Have Become the Responsibility of Government?

Government has three main areas of responsibility. These are making laws, **interpreting** laws, and providing services. Providing government for the people of Canada is challenging. In physical size, Canada is the second largest country in the world. The many landscapes, climates, and natural resources of our country affect the lifestyles of people throughout the country.

Life in a prairie city such as Brandon, Manitoba is different from life in the port community of Peggy's Cove, Nova Scotia. Both communities have some needs that are the same. One example of a similar need is clean drinking water. Other needs are different from one community to the other. Brandon, for example, might have an emergency flood plan in the event that the Assiniboine River overflows in spring or during heavy rains. Peggy's Cove might have a different emergency plan in the event of a fierce Atlantic storm.

Because of the size of our country and the many needs of the people, Canada has three levels of government. The federal government meets many of the needs that all communities have in common. One common need is a set of rules to protect the environment. Another common need is a postal system. Some needs, such as highways, are met through the provincial or territorial government.

Federal, provincial, and territorial governments have the authority to assign the responsibility for meeting some needs to local governments. Local governments may be given the responsibility for making laws (called **by-laws**) for the community. A local

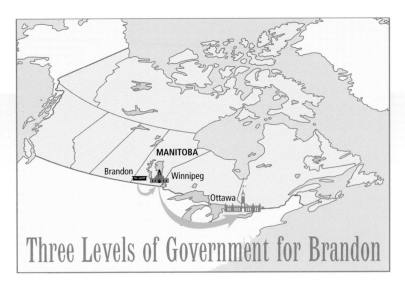

Three Levels of Government for Brandon

This map shows how one community is connected to Canada's three levels of government. The people of Brandon are affected by their own local government, the provincial government of Manitoba, and the federal government of Canada.

government may also be given responsibility for providing services in the community, such as the collection of garbage.

Government Work:
Making Laws

Living in a society means there is a need for good laws. Laws help large groups of people live together. Just as games don't work fairly without rules, communities have difficulty working without laws. All people are expected to follow the laws. This is the responsibility of every citizen. In Canada, people who believe a law is unfair or inappropriate can express their opinion to the government to try to change it.

Laws are made to help us meet our needs. Our laws show what we think is important and good for the people in our society. Look at the list below. Each example tells about a law we have in Canada. Why do you think each was made?

➤ Vehicles must be driven on the right-hand side of the road.
➤ No littering.

➤ July 1 is a national holiday.
➤ Children must attend school until the age of 16.
➤ People must wear seat belts in cars.
➤ No stealing.

Laws can change. In the middle 1800s and for many years, physical punishment was used in schools throughout our country. A student who told a lie might have hot mustard put on the tongue. Too much talking often resulted in a thick wooden stick being put in the mouth. A willow stick or a leather strap was used to hit the hands of children caught stealing or misbehaving. These consequences were used because people believed that pain would help change inappropriate behaviours. Today, most people do not believe physical punishment is helpful.

Sometimes new laws have to be written. When motor cars were invented, laws were written for the safety of people and animals. Here is a law that was written in one community. It talks about when motor vehicles can be driven.

> No person shall drive any such car or vehicle on or along any of the streets during the time between 30 minutes after sunset of any one day and 30 minutes prior to sunrise of the next following morning, unless attached to said car or vehicle there shall be three or more lighted lamps which shall be disposed as follows—two of such lamps shall show in front, one on each side or front corner of the vehicle, and the third in rear in position to cast light upon the number.

When a law is written and agreed to, it is put "on the books." This means it is recorded, showing the date the representatives voted and agreed to the law. New laws are recorded in a special book. This is where we get the expression "on the books."

This photograph shows Henry Ford driving a motor car produced by his American company in 1903. Why do you think early laws restricted the use of motor cars?

Your Turn

Life in Canadian towns and cities has changed since the motor car law described on page 28 was written.

1. Do you think this law has been changed or is still on the books?

2. What do you think should be included in a law about cars?

Government Responsibility:
Interpreting Laws

Laws are passed to govern behaviour of people in the society and for the protection of people and the Earth. Sometimes people do not abide by the laws. There are also times when people find themselves in conflict with another person over the interpretation or meaning of a part of the law.

In Canada, we have a court system. The role of the court is to interpret the laws. Our court system is based on the belief that a person is innocent until proven guilty. When a person is suspected of a crime, evidence must be gathered and evaluated. Only then will the case be heard in court.

Sometimes, innocence or guilt is decided by a judge; sometimes by a judge and jury. It is the role of the judges of the courts to decide the consequence when a person has been found guilty of breaking or violating the laws. When a crime is very serious, an offender may be sent to jail. Less serious crimes, such as littering, may result in a fine or in time for community service, or both. A person found guilty of writing graffiti on the walls of buildings may have to give 100 hours of community service. This service could involve taking care of parks or taking meals to elderly people. In some Aboriginal communities, responsibility for sentencing offenders is handled by Aboriginal Sentencing Circles. Sentencing Circles try to find ways to help the offender.

Word Origins

The word **judge** originates from an old Latin word *judex*. In ancient Rome, a person appointed to hear and make a decision about a case was called a judex.

The word was then adopted by the French as the word "juge." Around 1300 CE, the word "judge" appeared in the English language. At that time in England, a person's guilt or innocence was often determined by a physical trial or test. Someone accused of stealing might have to walk barefooted over red hot coals or plunge an arm into a pot of boiling water. If the person was unhurt, she or he was judged innocent; if he or she was hurt, they were judged guilty.

Eventually, this practice changed; innocence and guilt were decided by a judge and jury after they heard evidence. Like "judge" the word "jury" began with the Latin language of ancient Rome. It was adopted by the French and later became part of the English language.

Use the chart below to determine the kind of services represented in these photographs. Which level of government provides these services?

Government Responsibility:

Providing Services

Federal
transportation
fisheries
constitution
national parks
Indian Affairs
trade agreements
printing money
Trans-Canada Highway
patents of invention
criminal law making
environment
post office

Provincial
education
forestry, lands and wildlife
family and social services
provincial parks
health care and hospitals
agriculture
tourism
provincial inter-city highways
culture and multiculturalism
energy
environmental protection

Territorial
education
wildlife
housing
forest management
health care and hospitals
tourism
social services

Local
libraries
garbage collection
fire fighting
recreation
police service
transportation
public information
tax collection
parks
snow clearance
emergency medical services

In Canada we rely on our government to help us by providing services. Most responsibilities that affect meeting the needs of all Canadians have been given to the federal government. Some responsibilities, like tourism, are assigned to the provincial or territorial government. Other responsibilities, such as the location of crosswalks, are assigned to the local government.

The chart on the previous page outlines some of the needs of people living in Canada. The responsibility of providing services to meet each of these needs is assigned to different levels of government.

Your Turn

The chart lists only some of the many services provided by governments in Canada.

1. List the services your family used in the last week. Are there any services you listed that should be added to the chart?

2. Why do you think the responsibilities listed in the chart were assigned to each level of government?

3. Why do you think more than one level of government needs to be involved in highways and parks?

4. Are there other examples in the chart where you think levels of government are working together to meet a need?

How Does the Federal Government Ensure Canadians Are Equally Represented?

Canada has been organized into electoral areas called **constituencies** or ridings. People who live in a constituency have an elected representative who attends meetings of the federal government. These are called sessions of the House of Commons. In representative government, it is important that everyone is heard so that their needs can be met fairly, and people can be fairly represented.

In Canada, we use a system called the **census** process to gather a count of the population. From this count, our government organizes to be sure we have fair representation in an election. Every five years, population information is gathered in a census. This information is used for the country, the provinces and territories, and for cities, towns, and smaller communities. The government asks all people living in Canada to complete a census form on a specific day. The census is gathered by sending forms to homes, jails, shelters for homeless people, and any place that people might call home.

The census includes questions such as the ages of people, how people earn their living, what languages are spoken, how many people live in the same home, and whether the home is owned or rented.

Once the census has been taken, the information is studied. The government decides how many representatives each area needs. It is important for all people to be counted in order to get fair representation. In 1997, the federal government increased from 295 members to 301 members of the House of Commons. Census information showed that

The three levels of government participated in building the Trans-Canada Highway. The highway was completed in 1962 when the Roger's Pass (shown here) was finished.

The Trans-Canada Highway Story

Some services are best provided when more than one level of government works together in cooperation. The Trans-Canada Highway is an example of how one service was provided through different levels of government working for the people.

In the early 1900s Canadians knew a national road was needed to connect the country from east to west. This was an enormous project that took much longer than people had imagined. The geography of Canada made the project difficult and expensive. This was especially true of the section through the Rocky Mountains. The section of highway between Golden, British Columbia and Revelstoke, British Columbia can have more than 15 metres of snow in one winter. Special snow sheds had to be built to protect vehicles from avalanches. Another very expensive part of the highway was in Quebec where a tunnel had to be built under the St. Lawrence River. The tunnel is little more than one kilometre long and cost about $75 million dollars to build!

The Trans-Canada Highway was opened in 1962 when the Roger's Pass in the Rockies was completed. Canadians, with the help of ferries, could travel from St. John's, Newfoundland on Canada's east coast to Victoria, British Columbia on Canada's west coast. At a length of 7821 kilometres, the Trans-Canada is the longest national highway in the world.

Governments worked together to complete this great project. Federal and provincial governments shared the costs. Representatives of both levels of government worked to make sure that safe standards were set. One of these standards was trying to make sure the highway never crossed the railway unless absolutely necessary. Where the highway went through a community, local government was involved. Each provincial government supervised the building of its section of the highway.

Your Turn

1. What reasons do you think governments would have for cooperating to provide a service?

2. Can you think of other examples of services that might best be provided through cooperation?

This man has filled out his census form and is mailing it. The government makes various decisions based on the information gathered in the census.

the population had grown most in Ontario and British Columbia. As a result, these provinces were allowed a few more representatives.

Census information also gives the federal government an idea of the needs of Canadians. For example, if the census results show that most adult Canadians are unemployed, the federal government will consider spending money to create programs to increase employment. If most adult Canadians are employed, the government will use the money elsewhere.

Your Turn

1. Why do you think equal representation is important?

2. How would information gathered by the federal government be helpful to provincial, territorial, and local governments?

What Is the Role of an Elected Representative?

Elected representatives have the task of speaking for people in their riding. Rema Afech is an elected representative in one Canadian community. As you read what she has to say about her work, think about what kind of person would make a good representative.

I have been a representative for two years. When I was elected, I knew the work would be challenging. I knew I would always have to be learning new information, sometimes about things that weren't always really interesting to me. When I think about it now, I am amazed at how much I have learned. It takes a lot of time to do this part of my job! It's very important, though. How can I make a good decision if I don't have enough information?

The people I represent are very helpful. I learn a lot by listening to them. It is important for a representative to be a good listener. People have concerns that I might not even think of. They can also have some wonderful solutions to problems. When you are a representative, you have to hear different points of view. After all, how can you really represent the people if you don't know what they are thinking? I have learned not to judge other people's ideas, even when I don't agree.

One of the toughest parts of my job is what I call "putting away my own voice." You see, when you represent others, it is really their voice that must be heard. At least, it is the voice of the **majority** that must be heard. The idea of majority is difficult for some people to understand. It is not very often when every single person agrees on an issue. People do not always agree about what is best for everyone. Sometimes a decision cannot meet the needs of all people. When I speak for the majority, I speak for most of the people, but this doesn't usually mean everyone. Some people get very confused and upset when they are the minority. Sometimes they call or write and let me know how unhappy they are with the final decision. To me, it all has to do with **integrity.** I have to be honest with myself. When I know I have done my best to listen, learn, and speak in the best interests of the majority, I think I've done my best as their representative.

Your Turn

This representative says she speaks for the majority of her constituents. Imagine you are Rema Afech. The majority of people want you to vote to allow anyone under 16 years of age to buy cigarettes. You know the other representatives will vote in favour of this idea. You know that businesses will be happy to sell more cigarettes. But you do not believe that this is a good idea. What would you do?

Ideas for Further Understanding:

Who Is in the Minority?

A decision made by the majority, or the greater number of people, is not a decision of all people. Consider this situation:

Mr. Chu's grade 6 class is debating what to do for a special year-end activity. This is their last year at Glendale School. The students have come up with the following suggestions:

1. Go to a local amusement park that has a variety of rides and food kiosks.
2. Go on an overnight camping trip (boys only).

3. Order a "12 foot" mixed meat submarine sandwich and have a dance.
4. Bring a couple of favourite videos to school, make popcorn, and have everyone sleep over in the school gym.

In Mr. Chu's class, there were eight girls and fifteen boys. The girls were upset about the suggestion that the year-end activity would be something only boys could do. They also knew the boys would win if there was a vote. One of the girls made the suggestion about sleeping over at the school. Rachelle looked

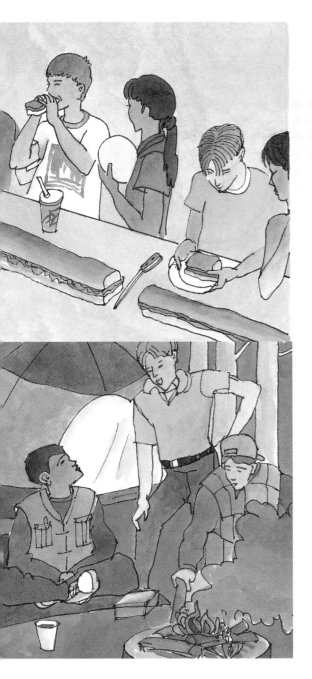

1. If this were your class, how would you feel about excluding some of the students in a year-end activity?

2. How would you feel about being excluded?

3. How do you think the class could use Mr. Chu's suggestion about the Charter of Rights and Freedoms?

The experience in Mr. Chu's class shows us that people can sometimes be in the minority because of who they are. The Charter of Rights and Freedoms is very helpful to government representatives as they work to make good decisions for all of the people they represent.

A person can also be in the minority because he or she has an idea, belief, or opinion that is different from most others. When this happens, a person in the minority has the opportunity to try to change the way the other people think. This can be done through organizing others who share similar ideas. In Chapter 7, you will learn several different ways to try to influence decisions.

Your Turn

1. Is there an issue in your school or community where people have different ideas or opinions? Explain.

2. Examine the majority opinion. Does it respect the rights of the minority?

3. Are there opportunities for the minority to influence the majority? Explain.

very uncomfortable when this suggestion was made. She could see a lot of the class liked the idea. In her religion, girls are not allowed to sleep away from their family.

Mr. Chu told the class about a special set of rules called "The Charter of Rights and Freedoms." He suggested that the ideas in the Charter might help the class make a decision that was good for everyone. In the Charter, many rights of people are protected. The Charter expects that people cannot be **discriminated against** because of their race, religion, **gender,** or age.

Chapter Focus

In Chapter 3, you learned that Canadian government is organized in three levels. These levels are the federal government, provincial or territorial government, and local government. This chapter examines how each level of government is organized to meet the three areas of responsibility: making laws, interpreting laws, and providing service.

As you read this chapter, consider these questions:

➤ How are the levels of government organized?

➤ Who are the leaders of government?

➤ How are territorial governments unique?

➤ How is the monarchy represented in government?

➤ What are political parties?

Chapter 4

Levels of Government

Vocabulary

administration –*n.* the management and supervision of local affairs by government officials

bilingual –*adj.* able to speak in two languages

commissioner –*n.* a representative in charge

currency –*n.* any form of money

empowered –*v.* to be given power

entrusted –*v.* to be counted on or believed in

judiciary –*n.* a system of courts

justice –*n.* the administration and process of the law

legislative –*adj.* having the power to make laws

lieutenant-governor –*n.* representative of the monarchy in the provinces

monarchy –*n.* government by a sovereign, such as a king or queen

municipal –*adj.* local, community level of government

Official Opposition –*n.* the second largest group of elected members of government who debate about the plans and actions of the political party or government in power

portfolio –*n.* specific responsibilities assigned to a member of government

rural –*adj.* in the country

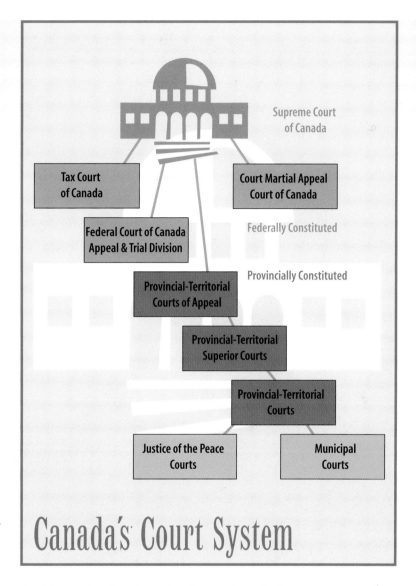

Canada's Court System

Federal Government:
How Is It Organized?

Federal government in Canada is organized into three main branches. This is because there are three main responsibilities of government.

...making laws

In federal government, the work of making laws is shared by the prime minister, the House of Commons, and the Senate. All laws must have a majority vote in the House of Commons and in the Senate. Laws also require the approval of the governor general.

The House of Commons consists of elected representatives. The Senate is made up of people who are appointed by the prime minister.

A citizen appointed to the Senate is called a senator. Usually, to become a senator, a person has been known by the prime minister for his or her work to make Canada better.

... interpreting laws

Laws are administered and interpreted through the courts. This is the work of the **judiciary**. Canada's federal judiciary is made up of the Supreme Court of Canada, the Federal Court, and the Provincial and Territorial Courts. The Supreme Court of Canada is the highest court in the country.

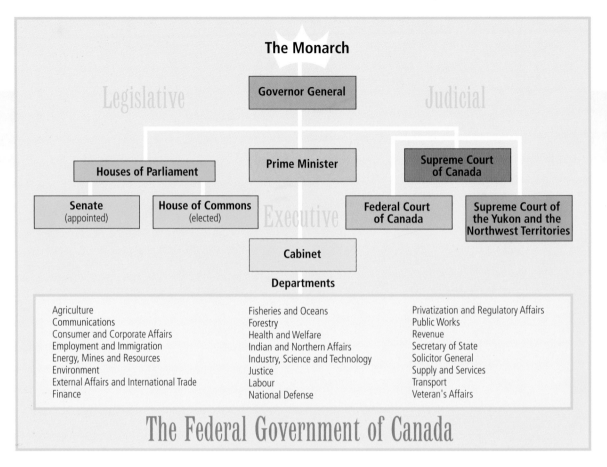

The Monarch

Governor General

Legislative

Houses of Parliament

Prime Minister

Judicial

Supreme Court of Canada

Senate (appointed)

House of Commons (elected)

Executive

Federal Court of Canada

Supreme Court of the Yukon and the Northwest Territories

Cabinet

Departments

Agriculture	Fisheries and Oceans	Privatization and Regulatory Affairs
Communications	Forestry	Public Works
Consumer and Corporate Affairs	Health and Welfare	Revenue
Employment and Immigration	Indian and Northern Affairs	Secretary of State
Energy, Mines and Resources	Industry, Science and Technology	Solicitor General
Environment	Justice	Supply and Services
External Affairs and International Trade	Labour	Transport
Finance	National Defense	Veteran's Affairs

The Federal Government of Canada

...providing services

There is also the **administration** or day-to-day work of the government. Federally, this is done by the prime minister and the cabinet. This group is also called the executive. Usually, these people are members of the House of Commons.

The prime minister and the cabinet make many of the decisions that affect our day-to-day lives. They make decisions about whether or not the east coast fishers can continue to fish for cod. They make decisions about whether or not we should change our **currency** from a two dollar bill to a two dollar coin. They make decisions about what kind of weapons private citizens can have.

To help do this important work, some cabinet ministers are asked by the prime minister to take a special assignment. This assignment is called a **portfolio.** One example of a portfolio is the work assigned to the Minister of Immigration.

The organization of our modern federal government continues to show our connections in history to British government and the **monarchy.** When Canada was made up of colonies, the head of government was the king or queen of Britain. Although the monarchy no longer has any real power in Canada, we remain connected. On the recommendation of the prime minister, the ruling monarch appoints a governor general who acts as a representative of her sovereignty in Canada. The governor general's role is to act as a symbol of our citizenship and for what all Canadians have in common. She or he is the honourary head of the federal government.

Your Turn

1. Why do you think decisions about our currency are best made by the federal government?

2. What might be the consequence if these decisions were made by provincial, territorial, or local governments?

The federal government is based in the Parliament Buildings in Ottawa, Ontario.

Federal Government:
Who Are the Leaders?

In Canada, the federal government is led by a prime minister. She or he is the leader of the political party that wins a majority in a federal election. The prime minister has the most powerful position in the government. Like all other Members of Parliament (also called MPs), the prime minister must be elected in his or her riding. Federal elections are usually held every four years. Members of Parliament from the whole country are elected. Every Canadian lives in a federal constituency (riding). Voters in each constituency elect a Member of Parliament to represent them in Ottawa and to help the prime minister make good decisions.

Provincial Governments:
How Are They Organized?

Provincial governments in Canada are organized much like the federal government. There are three branches for the three main areas of responsibility.

...making laws

Each province has a **Legislative** Assembly, which includes the premier and the provincial cabinet. The Legislative Assembly is a group of elected people responsible for making laws. It is the work of provincial legislators to make laws relating to **justice** in the province. For example, legislators decide what ages children must go to school. Legislators also decide what speed limits will be set for highways in the province.

Province	Title of Elected Representative	Name for Legislative Assembly
Alberta British Columbia Manitoba Saskatchewan New Brunswick Nova Scotia Prince Edward Island	Member of the Legislative Assembly (MLA)	Provincial Legislature
Ontario	Member of the Provincial Parliament (MPP)	Provincial Parliament
Quebec	Member of the National Assembly (MNA)	National Assembly
Newfoundland	Member of the House of Assembly (MHA)	House of Assembly

The legislative assembly and the elected representatives are given different names in different provinces.

The University of Regina is able to function partly because of financial support from Saskatchewan's provincial government.

... interpreting laws

Provincial courts are **entrusted** with the responsibility of interpreting and administering the by-laws of communities, the laws of the province, and the laws of Canada. For example, people who want to get married must get a licence from the provincial court. If a person owed you money and would not pay, you could take him or her to the small claims division of the provincial courts. A person accused of murder would be tried in a provincial court.

In some court cases, a person may be found guilty, but the lawyer believes the judgement of the court was in error. When this happens, an appeal may be filed with the Supreme Court of Canada.

...providing services

There is also the administration or day-to-day work of the government. Provincially, this is done by the premier and the cabinet. They make some of the decisions that affect our day-to-day lives. To help do this important work, some cabinet ministers are asked by the premier to take a special portfolio assignment. One example of a portfolio is the work assigned to the Minister of Education.

Your Turn

1. In schools, staff members often accept special responsibilities or assignments. These are similar to a portfolio. They may be done alone or with a committee. Talk to staff members in your school. Ask about the advantages and disadvantages of having staff members accept special assignments.

2. Why do you think our government leaders use a portfolio system for doing some of the work?

This photograph shows the chambers of the Legislative Assembly building in Yellowknife, Northwest Territories.

Provincial Governments:
Who Are the Leaders?

Provincial governments have an appointed, honourary head of government called a **lieutenant-governor**. However, provincial governments are actually led by a premier. The premier of a province is the leader of the political party that has the most people elected in a provincial election. Provincial elections are held at least every five years. Each province is divided into provincial ridings. Each riding elects one person to represent them in the provincial government.

How Are Territorial Governments Different?

In many ways the territorial governments work similarly to the provincial governments. Like the provinces, Canada's territories have a Legislative Assembly made up of elected representatives. Both territories have a leader of the Legislative Assembly. The leader is called the premier or the government leader.

The federal government also appoints a **commissioner** to serve as an honourary head of the government for each territory. The role of the commissioner is similar to that of the provincial lieutenant-governor.

In the Yukon Territory and the Northwest Territories, the Legislative Assemblies have been **empowered** by the federal government to make decisions. One exception is the right to make decisions about the control of some natural resources. The territories may make decisions about wildlife, but decisions about oil and natural gas are made by the federal government.

The Legislative Assembly in the Northwest Territories is unique because its members may debate in one of seven languages common in the North. Translators provide simultaneous translations for representatives if they do not understand the language being spoken. The Northwest Territories is also unique in that decisions are made in a consensus style of decision-making. This means that decisions are made after representatives have worked to find solutions with which everyone can agree.

Yukon Territory, like the provinces, uses a political party system of decision-making. In this case, after debate, people vote for or against a decision. The majority rules.

Your Turn

Try comparing a decision made by consensus with a decision made by a vote.

1. Identify two issues of interest to your class.

2. After discussion about the first issue, take a vote. Then, discuss the process. How long did the process take? Whose needs were satisfied? What different feelings did people have about the process? Record your observations.

3. Introduce and discuss the second issue. This time, try to identify a solution or final decision with which every member of the class can agree. After you have achieved a consensus decision, record your observations about this process. How long did the process take? Whose needs were satisfied? What different feelings did people have about the process?

4. List the advantages and disadvantages of each method of decision-making.

5. Are there times when you think one method would work better than the other? Why?

Profile:
Political Parties

People who run for office in federal, provincial, and some territorial elections are usually associated with a political party. People belonging to a political party generally have the same beliefs about how people should be governed. We have different political parties because people's opinions differ. Occasionally, some people run as "independents." These are people who wish to serve in government but do not choose to belong to one of the political parties. Some elections for local government are based on political parties. Vancouver is one city where people who run for office belong to political parties.

In Canada, there are several federal political parties. These include the Liberal Party, the Bloc Québécois, the Reform Party, the Progressive Conservative Party, and the New Democratic Party. The political party with the most elected candidates forms the federal government. After an election, the governor general will ask the leader of this party to become the prime minister. Elected representatives from the party with the second-most elected candidates become the **Official Opposition.**

Word Origins

Politics comes from the Greek words *polis* which means city-state, and *polites* which means citizen. Originally, the word had to do with the rights of a citizen. The word police has the same origin.

Local Government:
How Is It Organized?

Canada's third level of government is called local government or **municipal** government. It deals with the needs and concerns of the community in which it is located. Canada has many different types of communities. We have large cities, small towns, and villages. We have communities where cities have grown together. We also have **rural** communities where many of the people live on farms, ranches, or in the bush. There are other communities such as Native reserves and Hutterite colonies. The organization of the local government also depends on the size of the community.

Local governments work to make laws and provide services, but they are not empowered to interpret laws. People who are charged with breaking the by-laws of a community have their case heard in provincial or territorial court.

... making laws

Local governments are responsible for making laws for the people in the community. Local laws are called by-laws. Because communities are unique, by-laws in one community may be different from by-laws in another community. The elected council is responsible for making by-laws that will meet the needs of the community.

... providing services

Communities organize in a number of ways to provide services that the people need. In many communities, this work is assigned to a group of people who are organized into special departments. A large city might have a separate department that looks after emergency medical services, streets, and local parks and recreation.

What needs do you think local government fills in Inuvik, Northwest Territories?

Your Turn

How is the local government method for providing services similar to the method used by federal and provincial governments?

Many local governments in Canada meet in town or city halls. This photograph shows the city hall in Fredericton, New Brunswick.

Local Government:

Who Are the Leaders?

Every local government has a leader who is responsible for representing the best interests of the people. In cities and towns the leader is known as the mayor. On a reserve the leader is known as the chief. In a Hutterite colony, the leader is known as the preacher.

In local government, councillors, aldermen, or alderwomen work with the mayor to meet the needs of the community. Managers and elders work with the preacher in a Hutterite colony. On a reserve, the elected people who work with the chief are called councillors. The roles of members of local government are similar to the roles of members in other levels of government. The members debate issues, listen to people, suggest solutions to problems, and try to make the concerns of the people they represent heard. You will learn more about local government in Chapter 5.

Ideas for Gathering Information:

Using the Telephone and the Internet

To begin learning about local government, first discover the titles and names of the leaders. This information will help you to know who is doing what for you.

Telephone books usually have a government section. Telephone companies often print these government phone numbers on paper that is a different colour from the rest of the pages. In the government section of a phone book you can find phone numbers for the Government of Canada (federal), the provincial or territorial government, and the local government.

Canada is a **bilingual** country. This means there are two official languages spoken in Canada. These languages are English and French. In a phone book, Government of Canada numbers will be listed in English and in French. In many communities you will find the provincial and local government numbers listed in English but not in French.

Your Turn

1. What languages are used in your phone book for federal, provincial or territorial, or local phone numbers?

2. Where would you expect to see provincial, territorial, or local government numbers listed in French?

When you are planning to locate information by making phone calls, you need to be prepared before you dial the number. Write down the questions you want to ask. Be sure to have a pencil or pen and paper ready.

Good manners are always appropriate. Once the phone has been answered, state your name and the reason for your call. When answers are given, it is a good idea to repeat the information you have been given and to check for correct spelling. If the person answering the phone does not have the information, ask if he or she can suggest who you might call to find the information you need. When you have completed the call, be sure to thank the person who has helped you.

You can also find information about your government members on the Internet. Using a web search engine, you can locate websites for Canada's federal government as well as each provincial and territorial government. Many Canadian cities have their own government websites, too. In each website you will find a list of government members, their constituencies, duties, addresses, phone numbers, and usually their biographies. You will also find their Email addresses and you will be given the opportunity to leave an Email message right away.

Use your local phone book or the Internet to help you research the following information about government leaders who are working for your community.

Federal Government:

➤ Find out your prime minister's name and his or her political party.

➤ Find out your Member of Parliament's name and his or her political party.

Provincial or Territorial Government:

➤ Find out your premier or government leader's name and political party.

➤ Find out the name of your Member of the Legislative Assembly and his or her political party. (If you live in Quebec, this will be a Member of the National Assembly. If you live in Ontario, this will be a Member of the Provincial Parliament. If you live in Newfoundland, this will be a Member of the House of Assembly.)

Local Government:

➤ Find out your community leader's name and title.

Chapter Focus

Local government is located in your own community. Local government is empowered by the provincial or territorial government to carry out a variety of activities. In local government, the representatives are citizens who live in the community. The issues and services specifically relate to the community. Because the people in communities across Canada have many different needs, local government looks slightly different from one community to another. Although local governments are organized in different ways, the work that is done is very similar. This chapter will explore some ways that local governments can be organized.

As you read this chapter, consider these questions:

➤ How are municipalities classified?

➤ Why are by-laws made?

➤ How do local governments meet people's needs?

➤ Are all local governments the same?

➤ How do local governments raise money?

Chapter 5

Local Government

Vocabulary

administer –v. to manage and supervise local affairs

annually –adv. once a year

civil service –n. people directly employed by government to provide services

classify –v. to arrange according to characteristics

confluence –n. the place where two or more rivers join and flow together

cul-de-sac –n. a dead end street

dignitaries –n. important or famous people

district –n. a part of a region

economy –n. the management of the resources of a country, community, or business

enacts –v. makes into law

hospitality –n. friendly treatment

incorporated –adj. officially a community established under provincial or territorial law

infraction –n. a breaking of a law

liable –adj. to be responsible by law

ordinance –n. a rule or law made by authority

reeve –n. an elected community leader in a rural area

repeal –v. to cancel or do away with

summary conviction –n. a quick judgement

uphold –v. to agree with and enforce

urban –adj. in the city

Saint John, New Brunswick was the first incorporated municipality in Canada.

How Are Municipalities Classified?

The provincial or territorial government empowers communities to organize local governments. A community that has been empowered to form a local government is called a municipality. In 1785, Saint John, New Brunswick became the first **incorporated** municipality in what later became Canada. It was set up under the colony of New Brunswick's laws.

To be incorporated, a community must have:

➤ boundaries (often called city or town limits)

➤ a council to make decisions on behalf of the local residents

➤ ways to carry out decisions for the good of the community

Provinces and territories **classify** local communities. Communities can be classified according to the population size and the number of properties needed in the community. Each province and territory uses different population and property numbers when they classify their communities.

A hamlet is one classification of a community. To be a hamlet, a community must have at least five buildings which are occupied. A hamlet must also have a name and it must

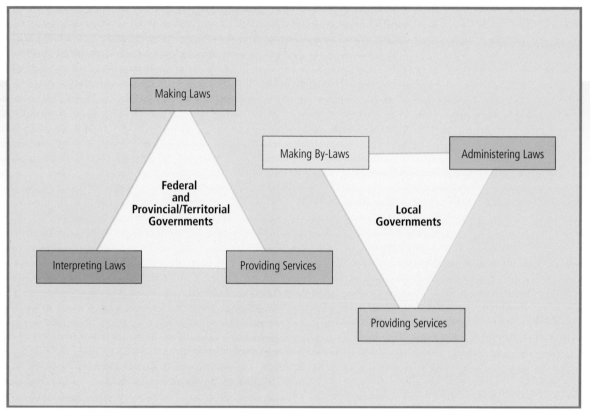

have boundaries. It is usually an unincorporated **district** within a larger rural municipality. The next larger community classification is a village. Towns, cities, counties, and municipal districts are other classifications.

The responsibilities entrusted to a local government depend on the classification of the community. The classification is based on the land size as well as the population size of the community. The larger the community, the more responsibilities it has. In a city, for example, the community pays people to carry out the work of the municipal government. In smaller communities, the provincial or territorial government may provide some of the services for the community.

Your Turn

Find out how your province or territory classifies communities.

How Is Local Government Organized?

Local governments work together with federal and provincial or territorial governments. One job all three levels of government have is creating laws. Federal, provincial, and territorial courts interpret these laws for all levels of government. Local government does not interpret laws, but it does **administer** them. The above chart shows how the work of local government is similar to the work of other levels of government.

Local governments are organized in many different ways. The style of government usually depends on the size of the community. In most local governments, the leader is elected to office. This leader is usually called a mayor, although in some municipal districts, the leader may be called a **reeve.** Along with a mayor or reeve, a number of council members are also elected. The mayor or reeve chairs meetings of the elected council.

Working with other elected officials to

The local government in Calgary, Alberta was responsible for hosting the 1988 Winter Olympics. This photograph shows the opening ceremonies.

make decisions for the good of the community is an important part of the duties of a mayor or reeve. They debate issues such as how to spend money, how to provide public transportation, and whether to allow gambling. A mayor or reeve also performs official functions at special events. He or she might make a speech at the opening of a new school. If a city hosts a major event like the Olympic Games, the mayor is expected to make speeches, be part of the opening and closing ceremonies, and greet important guests who are visiting the event.

Local governments differ in the way the day-to-day managing of services is done. In some local governments, council members work directly with the departments or people hired to provide a service. In other local governments, a city manager works with service departments, following the wishes of the council and keeping the council informed of the work being done by the service department. Other local governments have a number of commissioners who work with service departments in much the same way as city managers do.

Some communities do not have a local government. Communities in which a small number of people are separated by large distances are called improvement districts or rural municipalities. In these areas where it is difficult for people to gather, the provincial or territorial government may appoint an administrator or director. Citizens who live in the district or area are then elected to an advisory council. The administrator and the council meet to discuss the needs of the people. The administrator then reports back to the provincial or territorial government, which makes the final decisions and provides service to the people of the district.

Word Origins

The word **reeve** has been used to describe local leaders since the early days of Nova Scotia and Prince Edward Island. A "hog reeve" had the important job of finding stray pigs, deciding the costs of property damage that they had caused, and making sure their owners paid up!

Local Government:
Making By-Laws

Laws that are made in local communities are called by-laws. By-laws are made because of a specific need in the community. They are intended to make life safer and better for people living in the community. Sometimes, communities have similar needs. It is possible to see many communities with a by-law about the same issue. One example would be a by-law about the speed limit in school zones. Communities write a by-law about school zones because they want their children to be safe. Because communities are unique, many other by-laws are different and are made to meet the special needs of the community.

Examining old by-laws is an interesting way to learn about how by-laws work for a community.

When a by-law is no longer useful, the council of the local government can remove or cancel a by-law through a process called **repealing** a by-law. As communities grow and change, elected officials of local government must also respond to the need for new by-laws. These by-laws might relate to increased

Look at this photograph and discuss why you think Calgary would enact a bill restricting the use of bridges in 1913.

traffic which brings congestion, pollution, or safety concerns. A community might be concerned about the use of skateboards on downtown sidewalks or dogs running off leash in parks.

Your Turn

1. What does by-law #1504 tell you about life in Calgary in 1913?

2. What might have been happening that created a need for this by-law?

3. This by-law remained on the books until it was repealed in 1958. Why do you think this by-law was repealed?

4. What changes can you imagine were occurring in Calgary during the 1950s?

5. What might happen to a community if old by-laws were left active on the books?

6. What issues are of concern in your community?

7. Try contacting a representative of your local government to find out if new by-laws are planned for your community.

By-Law #1504:
Relating to the Use of Bridges

The Council of the City of Calgary **enacts** as follows:

1. No person shall hereafter ride or drive on any bridge within or partially within the City of Calgary at a rate faster than a walk.

2. No person shall hereafter cross upon any bridge within or partially within the City of Calgary at one time any greater number of horses, cattle, sheep or pigs than as follows:

    Horses, 10.
    Cattle, 10.
    Sheep, 50.
    Pigs, 50.

3. No person shall drive any such animal at a rate faster than walking.

4. Any person guilty of an **infraction** of this by-law or any part thereof shall be **liable** on **summary conviction** to the penalties described in section 149 of **Ordinance** 33 of 1893 of the Northwest Territories.

DONE AND PASSED IN COUNCIL THIS 5th DAY OF MAY, 1913.

Local Government:
Administering By-Laws

Local governments employ police officers to ensure the community by-laws are followed. Some by-laws are rules that everyone in the community is expected to know and follow. These are by-laws about community safety. Speed limits are one of these by-laws.

By-laws also help to improve life in the community. For example, a by-law might protect public property, such as parks. There may be a Parks Department with people hired to ensure parks are clean, the grass is cut, and dead trees are removed. By-laws might protect public health by ensuring that garbage does not spread around the streets. A special department may be responsible for making sure garbage is collected and removed to a landfill site or dump.

The Halifax police are responsible for enforcing the city's by-laws in order to keep the community safe.

Profile:
What Happens When People Have Different Points of View About the Law?

Street hockey has been a favourite pastime in Edmonton for decades.

Someone complained to city police in Edmonton, Alberta about children playing street hockey every night after school on a **cul-de-sac**. Of the 18 homes in the area, most had children who joined in the fun. Some parents joined in, too. One person, however, did not like the activity. He complained to the police.

The unhappy citizen who complained knew about local by-law 12:12. This by-law states, "No person shall play any game on any roadway or alley in the city." This meant the police were required to **uphold** the by-law. They informed the children and their parents that unless they stopped the street play, they would be fined $35 each for violating the by-law.

Your Turn

1. Why do you think this by-law was passed?

2. What might happen if the by-law was repealed?

3. Many of the children and their parents were disappointed that the game had to stop. Do you think the person who made the complaint was doing the right thing or the wrong thing? Why?

Sydney, Nova Scotia is known for its steel industry.

In the 1800s, people came to the Yukon to look for gold. A community called Dawson quickly grew to provide services for the gold prospectors.

Municipal Services

police

disaster services

day-care

centre for the arts & culture

cemeteries

public transportation

garbage collection & disposal

municipal planning & zoning

fire

convention centre

electricity

land, housing

roads, streets, sidewalks, & lighting

storm sewers & drainage

parks

recreational facilities & programs

telephone system

airports

sanitary sewage & treatment

ambulance

family & community support services

water supply & distribution

public housing

libraries

Local Government:

Providing Services

Local governments can provide many different services. Look at the list on the left of this page. Can you identify which of these services are being provided by local government in your community?

As you examine the following Canadian communities, think about what services would be most important for them.

Sydney, Nova Scotia is a small seaport city of 21 000 people. It is located on the tip of Cape Breton Island in the Atlantic Ocean. Being so close to the ocean, Sydney receives heavy rainfall and fierce winter storms. Sydney is also located by the largest coal field in eastern Canada. Sydney is known for coal mining and for its steel industry. Being a seaport means Sydney has heavy traffic from trucks bringing the coal and steel to sea-going ships. What would local government representatives have to think about as they worked to provide services to this community?

Dawson City, Yukon Territory is a town of 1900 people located at the **confluence** of the Yukon and Klondike Rivers. In the late 1800s, thousands of people arrived at Dawson to search for gold. This period of time is an important part of Canada's history. The federal government has named Dawson an historical site. Although the gold rush ended nearly 100 years ago, many tourists visit Dawson every year. Every summer, the town hosts a celebration called "Discovery Days." Tourism is very important to the **economy** of Dawson. When tourism is an important business in a

People from Edmundston and Madawska work in a large pulp and paper mill. Both communities are joined by an international bridge.

Montreal is one of the ports on the St. Lawrence Seaway. The seaway is an essential route for ships to transport goods to and from Canada.

community, what might local government representatives have to think about?

Montreal, Quebec is a large city of more than one million people. It is located at the confluence of the St. Lawrence River and the Ottawa River. Even though it is located more than 1600 kilometres inland from the Atlantic Ocean, Montreal is one of Canada's major ports. Ships travel up and down the deep St. Lawrence River and seaway, carrying goods in and out of the country. Montreal is a city of manufacturing and trade. It is also a banking centre for Canada. Much of Canada's business takes place in Montreal.

Many languages are spoken in Montreal. More than two-thirds of the people who live in Montreal speak French. English is the other major language. In Montreal, you will find some people who only speak English, some who only speak French, and others who are bilingual and speak both languages. You will also find people who speak English and Cantonese or French and Spanish. How might language affect the work of the local government?

Edmundston, New Brunswick is a French-speaking community. It is located in a valley at the confluence of the Madawska River and the St. John River. During the early years of Canada's exploration, voyageurs and Native peoples travelled by river from the Bay of Fundy to the St. Lawrence River. Today, the St. John River forms part of the border between Canada and the United States.

An international bridge has been built which joins Edmundston to the American city of Madawska, Maine. The people from both cities work in one large pulp and paper mill. The company which owns the mill built pipes across the river to transport pulp. The mill provides work for the people, but river

Name the kinds of services being supplied by local government in these photographs. Why do you think these services are better provided by local governments than by private businesses?

pollution is a concern. How might the pulp and paper mill affect the work of the local government?

In each of these Canadian communities, there is a need for government that works closely with and for the people. Each community needs representatives who understand the needs of the community. When we live together in communities, we can help each other and be efficient by providing services for each other. There are some services, like fire protection, that everyone needs. When everyone needs a service, we often turn to our local government to help provide the service for us. This part of the local government is called the **civil service.**

How Do Local Governments Raise Money?

Local governments must raise money to keep operating. People who work for the government need to be paid. Money is needed to provide services. Equipment like fire engines and garbage trucks must be bought. Local governments also raise money for such things as library books, flowers that are planted in public parks, and police uniforms.

A local government has four main ways of raising money: property taxes, user fees, licences, and transfer payments.

Property taxes are the way local governments raise most of their money. People who own land pay money to the local government. A business or industry pays the highest property tax. Taxes for a highrise apartment are higher than taxes for a house. The rate of taxes also depends on where the land is located, what the property is used for, and the value of the buildings.

Another way of raising money is through user fees. When you pay for a library card or buy a pass to use the local swimming pool, you are helping pay for local government.

When people buy a licence to operate a business, drive a taxi, ride their bicycles, or own a pet, the licence fee is paid to the local government.

Local governments can also receive money from federal, provincial, or territorial governments. This money is called a transfer payment. This happens when local government provides essential services like education.

The quality of services a local government is able to provide depends on how much money the community is able to raise.

Your Turn

1. List user fees that help fund your local government.

2. Look around your community. Are there services you do not have, but would like?

3. How might your community raise money to provide these services?

This photograph of Saskatoon in the 1960s shows a residential zone and an industrial zone. Can you identify them? Identify the school in this picture. What clues helped you to identify it?

What Is the Role of Local Government in Planning for the Future?

Most Canadian communities grow and change with time. As local governments provide services, make laws, and administer laws, thought must be given to the future. Thinking about the future includes planning for how to use the land. Rules about how land can be used are called zoning rules. In a community, some areas are zoned "residential" which means only homes can be built. Other areas are zoned "commercial" for businesses, or "industrial" for industries. Local government planning departments try to help communities grow and change in positive ways.

In 1966, Saskatoon, Saskatchewan developed a plan for future city development. In the plan it stated that:

➤ neighbourhoods will be built according to the need for schools
➤ no house will be farther than 0.3 kilometre from the neighbourhood elementary school

- neighbourhoods will be joined into districts that are big enough to need one high school
- neighbourhoods will have open park spaces
- neighbourhoods will have land for businesses that provide services
- no house will be farther than 525 metres from a bus stop

Your Turn

1. As you look at these ideas, what do you think was most important or valued by the Saskatoon planners in 1966?

2. How do you think Saskatoon might be changing or adding to this plan today?

3. What do you think would be most important or valued in a plan for a community that is moving into the twenty-first century?

4. Find out if your local government has a planning department. Ask for information that explains how your community is planning for the future. If possible, invite a community planner to speak to your class.

Word Origins

The title of **alderman** comes from the old Anglo-Saxon word *ealde* which later became the word "old." The Anglo-Saxons attached ealde to the front of another noun to show special honour or rank. A chief, a prince, or a tribal leader would then be known as an *ealdorman.* Through time, in families, this word became grandfather. In positions of leadership, it became alderman.

Today, many of our elected officials are women. Many local governments are changing the title to councillor, or to alderwoman when the elected representative is a woman.

How Is Local Government Organized in a City?

The population of our country continues to grow as people from all over the world decide to make Canada their home. For many people, cities have become a popular place to live. Cities provide a variety of jobs. Most large universities are located in cities. Hospitals help people with a variety of health care needs. For many people, the variety of entertainment, shopping, and services makes cities an attractive place to live. More and more people are choosing the **urban** lifestyle.

As urban communities have grown, local governments have had to change the way the work is done in order to respond to the growing needs of communities. Urban communities have a city council. In the early years, mayors were elected **annually.** Because the job of mayor is more complex today, mayors are usually elected for a three-year term of office.

Cities are divided into areas that are served by an elected representative. Often these areas are called wards. The number of areas or wards determines how many representatives will be elected to the city council to work with the mayor. The elected official for a ward is usually called an alderman or a city councillor. As a city grows, the boundaries of the wards may change and new areas will be added. This means that the number of elected representatives may increase. The size of each ward is decided by the number of people who live in the area. For fair and equal representation on council, a city organizes the wards according to the number of people who live there.

One of the best ways to learn how your local government works is by attending a council meeting.

Ireland's Eye was a small village that was home to cod fishers and their families. The village was abandoned in the 1950s because modern fish plants were being built elsewhere.

What Happens When a Community Dies?

Communities grow and change in different ways. How might a local government have helped the people of Ireland's Eye during its time of change?

Ireland's Eye was one of more than 1000 tiny outport villages in Newfoundland. Outports were home to many of Canada's cod fishers and their families. Most of the outports received services from the provincial government.

In the late 1940s, modern fish plants were being built in larger communities on Newfoundland's coast. People in the outport communities could not compete. Many feared they would have to leave the outports to make a living.

The provincial government wanted to save money. If the outports closed, money could be saved in services. The new fish plants also needed workers. The provincial government offered families money if they would leave their communities. As long as everyone in a community agreed to leave, a family would be paid between $300 and $600 to move. By 1954, more than 40 outports had become ghost towns. In 1965, the federal government became involved. If 75 per cent of a community agreed to move, every household was paid $1000, with an additional $200 for each person in the family.

Calgary:

Case Study of an Urban Community

Calgary, Alberta is one example of an urban community. Use the following brochure to examine ways your community is similar to or different from Calgary. If you live in Calgary, compare your city with another Canadian community.

Your Turn

1. How does local government operate in your community?

2. In what ways is your government's work similar to the work done by Calgary's government? How is it different?

3. Explain why you think your local government is similar to and different from Calgary's.

4. How do you think governments should inform the community of their work?

WELCOME
to the CITY of CALGARY

The Saddledome is Calgary's main sports arena.

Population Growth

Dominion Census (1891-1921, 1941), Civic Census (1931, 1951-1991).

Identity

Many local governments identify symbols to represent their community. These symbols may be on official pins, flags, and letters. These symbols tell a story about the community. Cities may have special songs, mascots, or floral emblems, too.

Calgary's flag was officially accepted in October 1983. The white Stetson cowboy hat has been worn by Calgarians since Calgary was incorporated as a town in 1884. For nearly 40 years, the Stetson has been given to visiting **dignitaries** from around the world. It is a symbol of the **hospitality** and spirit of Calgary. The large letter C stands for Calgary in its one hundredth year. It also stands for character, culture, change, and charm, words which are believed to represent Calgary.

Description

Calgary is an urban community with a population of about 800 000. The Bow River and the Elbow River flow through the city. Winter weather often begins late in October and continues until March. Often, Calgary experiences heavy snowfall. The city is known for its warm chinook winds which can raise the temperature by many degrees. Calgarians tell stories about wearing mittens and scarves in the morning, and splashing in puddles in the afternoon.

Agriculture, oil, and natural gas are Calgary's main industries. Much of the business for these industries is done in highrise buildings located downtown.

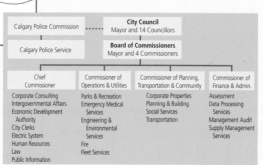

Calgary Police Commission	City Council Mayor and 14 Councillors		
Calgary Police Service	Board of Commissioners Mayor and 4 Commissioners		
Chief Commissioner	Commissioner of Operations & Utilities	Commissioner of Planning, Transportation & Community	Commissioner of Finance & Admin.
Corporate Consulting Intergovernmental Affairs Economic Development Authority City Clerks Electric System Human Resources Law Public Information	Parks & Recreation Emergency Medical Services Engineering & Environmental Services Fire Fleet Services	Corporate Properties Planning & Building Social Services Transportation	Assessment Data Processing Services Management Audit Supply Management Services

Model of Government

Calgary uses a council-board of commissioners model of government. Every three years, Calgary elects a mayor. Calgary has been divided into 14 wards so 14 councillors are elected at the same time as the mayor. Together, the mayor and councillors form the city council.

Because Calgary is large and growing rapidly, the local government has organized services into four main areas. Each area has a commissioner who is responsible for the day-to-day work of the departments. One department is the Engineering and Environmental Services Department: Streets Division. This department is responsible for duties such as street cleaning, pothole patching, street, lane and sidewalk repairs, local improvements, driveway crossings, and construction sites.

The commissioner shares new information and needs with the council, gives advice to council when asked, and keeps council advised about how work is progressing. City council uses this information to establish by-laws, give direction to the commissioners about the work of the departments, and to plan for the future.

City council appoints nine people to a special group called the police commission. Two of the people are elected councillors. The other seven are citizens. The police commission works with the police department.

Ideas for Gathering & Presenting Information:

Profiling Your Community

Create a profile of government in your community. Your task should begin with establishing a plan. Decide on the audience who will be interested in learning about government in your community. Identify what kind of information they will need. You might want to talk to your audience before you begin collecting data. Find out if they have questions they would like answered. Find out where you can find the information.

Once you have gathered your data, you will need to follow a number of steps to examine and organize the information.

... organizing information

Sort and classify your information into categories under main headings. This will help you determine if you have collected enough basic information.

... analyzing data

Check your data carefully. Be sure it is accurate by checking the facts in several information sources. If you are collecting opinions, you must check with many sources before you can use expressions like "most of the people."

... interpreting data

Once you have completed data collection, decide what format you will use to share the information. You might consider a brochure, a television "info-mercial," or a billboard poster. The format you choose will help you decide on how to interpret the data. If you are choosing a brochure, you may want to use graphs or charts to share the information. On a billboard poster, selecting key words will be important.

When you are communicating with others, standards are important. Information that is poorly presented may not be communicated. Before you begin, take time to examine examples of the format you are planning to use. How is it organized? What makes it noticeable? Why do you like it? By examining successful examples, you can make decisions about different ways of presenting information. You can also see how to be successful in producing your own quality project.

Chapter Focus

In Chapter 5, you read that local government in Canada does not work the same way everywhere. Although people's physical needs are the same, government is affected by many factors, including geography, climate, population, history, and culture. Rapid growth can mean changes to the local government, too. Whatever form of government a community uses, it must work to protect and improve life for the people it serves.

This chapter is a series of profiles of communities shaping local government to meet their needs.

As you read this chapter, consider these questions:

➤ Why are local governments organized in different ways?

➤ How do different communities organize for local government?

➤ What do communities need to consider when choosing a form of local government?

➤ How do we form responsible opinions?

Chapter 6

Profiling Government in Unique Communities

The provincial government of Ontario urged six municipalities to become one Toronto Megacity. From left to right, this photograph shows some of the people involved in the decision: Mayor Barbara Hall of Toronto, Mayor Doug Holyday of Etobicoke, Ontario Liberal leader Dalton McGuinty, and Mayor Frank Faubert of Scarborough.

Vocabulary

amalgamate –*v.* to combine two or more things, such as municipalities, into one

awareness –*n.* to know or realize

baptized –*v.* to be named in a religious ceremony; to become part of a religious community

bill –*n.* a draft of a proposed law presented for approval by a legislative body

borough –*n.* another name for a town or city that has its own local government

employment –*n.* the work a person is paid to do

image –*n.* an appearance or impression

metropolitan –*adj.* a major city and its suburbs; a form of local government based on several municipalities joining together to form a large urban area

moratorium –*n.* an official delay

ordained –*v.* to be appointed to an official position

probationary –*adj.* having to do with a trial or test period

regulations –*n.* laws or rules

sanitarium –*n.* a hospital for resting and healing

status –*n.* recognized standing or position in a community; official recognition

Toronto:

Government for a Megacity

Toronto, the capital city of Ontario, is known as a **metropolitan** area. A metropolitan area is made up of one or more cities and towns. Metropolitan Toronto is made up of six municipalities.

> **Municipalities of Metropolitan Toronto**
> City of Toronto
> City of North York
> City of Scarborough
> City of York
> City of Etobicoke
> **Borough** of East York

Metropolitan Toronto is an example of how physical geography can influence population growth. The waterway of the Great Lakes to the St. Lawrence River provides a shipping route to the Atlantic Ocean. Many industries have located in this region of Canada because of this good shipping route. Wherever large industries are located, there is a variety of **employment** for people.

The six municipalities did not always belong to Metropolitan Toronto. They started as separate communities. When they grew in size,

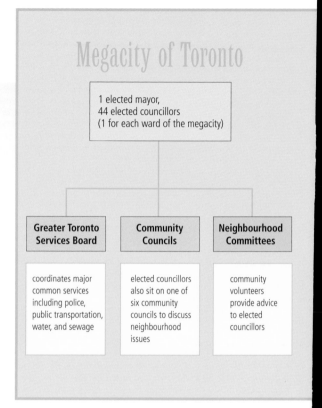

Level One

Metropolitan Council (Metro)
responsibilities include police, ambulance, social services, major roads, garbage disposal, taxis, traffic lights, water, the subway, nursing homes, the zoo

City of Toronto	City of North York	City of York	City of Scarborough	City of Etobicoke	Borough of East York
mayor, 7 metro council members	mayor, 7 metro council members	mayor, 2 metro council members	mayor, 6 metro council members	mayor, 4 metro council members	mayor, 1 metro council members

Level Two

Six Municipalities
responsibilities include garbage pickup, fire departments, local streets, local parks, public health

City of Toronto	City of North York	City of York	City of Scarborough	City of Etobicoke	Borough of East York
mayor, 14 council members	mayor, 14 council members	mayor, 8 council members	mayor, 14 council members	mayor, 12 council members	mayor, 8 council members

1 elected mayor,
44 elected councillors
(1 for each ward of the megacity)

Greater Toronto Services Board	Community Councils	Neighbourhood Committees
coordinates major common services including police, public transportation, water, and sewage	elected councillors also sit on one of six community councils to discuss neighbourhood issues	community volunteers provide advice to elected councillors

These maps and charts show Metropolitan Toronto and the new Toronto Megacity.

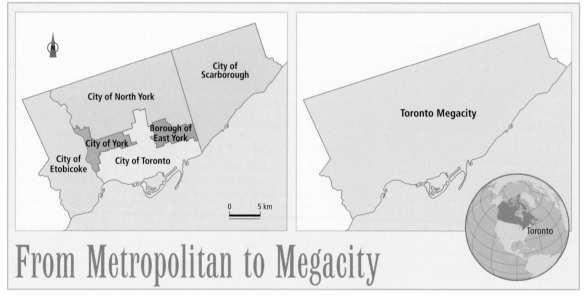

From Metropolitan to Megacity

their borders grew closer together. In the early 1950s, local leaders realized the six municipalities needed to work together to meet the needs of the people. Together, there were more than one million people living in the area. The leaders realized that transportation was a problem they could work on together. They wanted to build a better road system. They wanted to build a subway system, too.

In 1953, the form of local government changed to help meet these needs. The provincial government formed an area-wide government, and called it the Metropolitan Council, or "Metro." Metro was made up of the mayors of each community and a group of elected councillors. This Council took over responsibilities for services such as roadways, water, and the subway system. Other services, such as the police, became the responsibility of the metropolitan government later.

The six communities believed it was also important to maintain their own local governments to meet some needs. Each municipality wanted their own mayor and council. This level of local government was elected from people who lived in the municipality. The mayor sat on the local government, and also represented the community on the Metropolitan Council. Each municipality elected a council to work with the mayor. Until 1988, many local councillors served their municipalities and also served on the Metro Council.

The "Metropolitan Toronto" chart on the previous page shows how Metropolitan Toronto and its six municipalities were organized into the two levels of local government. For more than 40 years, local government in Toronto was organized in this way.

The provincial government began urging the municipalities of Toronto to **amalgamate** into a "megacity" by 1998. The megacity would replace the six municipal governments and Metro with one local government. The chart "Megacity of Toronto," and map "From Metropolitan to Megacity," on the previous page show how the provincial government wanted to organize the megacity.

In April 1997, the **bill** proposing the amalgamation became law. The provincial government then set up the City of Toronto Transition Team, consisting of six municipal politicians. The purpose of the Transition Team is to define further the structure of the new city, using the opinions of Metro citizens and elected representatives. The team's proposals are to be implemented in 1998. The megacity's official name is the City of Toronto.

There are many different opinions about the amalgamation. Some people like it. Others do not. Below are some of the arguments for and against amalgamation.

Your Turn

1. What do you think of the provincial government's plan for local government in Metropolitan Toronto? Give reasons for your answer.

2. Do you live in a part of Canada where a number of communities are located closely together? Explore reasons for and against creating a "megacommunity" where you live.

3. Be a news watcher. Watch the newspaper, radio, and television for information on how local government is working in Toronto.

For Amalgamation

➤ Amalgamation will save money currently spent on running two levels of local government.

➤ Amalgamation already began when Metropolitan Toronto started providing 75 per cent of the services.

➤ It is easier for a larger city to host big events such as the Olympics and World Expositions.

➤ Amalgamation will encourage cooperation among the communities rather than competition.

Against Amalgamation

➤ The megacity still will have six community councils. This new form of government will be as expensive as the old form.

➤ Only a person with plenty of money will be able to run for mayor because it could cost as much as $500 000 to mail one campaign flyer to every home.

➤ "Neighbourhood committees" will consist of volunteers who will not necessarily represent the community.

The people of Banff, Alberta elect a mayor and six councillors to run their local government. There is also an appointed town manager. This photograph shows the new town hall being built in Banff.

Banff:
A Town Inside a National Park

Like many towns throughout Canada, Banff has a local government made up of elected officials. The people of Banff elect a mayor and six councillors to run their local government. A town manager is appointed by the council. Government is unique in Banff because of the location of the community.

The town of Banff is located in Canada's oldest national park. For more than a century, Banff National Park has been one of Canada's major tourist spots. Three and a half million visitors from all over the world visit Banff every year.

When you drive into Banff, you are greeted with street upon street of shops and restaurants. All buildings are carefully designed to keep the mountain **image**. Tour buses can be seen on the streets loading and unloading weary travellers with their own mountain of baggage. It is hard to believe that this busy shopping area is in a national park.

The National Parks Act of 1930 established the main purpose of a national park as protecting the environment. It was hoped that national parks would maintain and preserve the natural environment forever.

Some people believe that the growth of towns and villages in national parks is harming the environment. In Banff, parking lots, streets, and buildings are on land that once was forest. Other people point out that, in Banff, new buildings are put on land that has already been used by people for years. This way, Banff is not taking over more natural forest land.

Discussing the Issues:
Should Towns in National Parks Be Allowed to Grow?

People view issues and form opinions in many different ways. Usually, people begin by expressing a concern. A concern begins when you feel that what you see happening is not quite right, good, or fair. Often when people are facing an issue, they talk to friends and neighbours. They try to express what is concerning them, and they listen to other points-of-view. We can learn a great deal by listening to each other.

The following people live in a community in a national park that faces similar problems to Banff. Examine some of the concerns and points-of-view they are expressing.

Frank Cardinal, *park warden*

Have you heard what is being done? Last spring the antlers of many bull elk were removed. This was done to protect people from being harmed by the antlers if an elk charged them. The problem is, the elk need those antlers during mating season. When two elk charge each other to fight for a female, they fight with their antlers. An elk without antlers could be seriously injured or even killed.

Nykkole Slater, *tourist*

This town is here because of tourism. This town provides work for many people. Look at all the students who get summer jobs here.

Last summer, park wardens started a controlled forest fire. This was done to help the forest continue with new growth. Some pine cones need high heat in order to open and let out the seed! I thought all forest fires were bad, but I guess this has to be done sometimes. My aunt said when a forest fire is planned, it is called a "controlled burn."

Because of the fire, one of the campgrounds had to be closed. Some people felt their summer holiday was ruined because of it. The smoke was so thick it burned our eyes and throats. We went home early. Tourists may stop coming if they think their holidays might be spoiled.

Scott Ferguson, *retired citizen*

I know that in 1994, the federal Environment Minister was concerned about the growth of the town. He put a **moratorium** on development in the area and ordered a study to assess the effects of growth and tourism on the wildlife and the habitat. We live in a beautiful part of the world here. What we have could not be easily replaced. What if all the animals really are at risk? I think we have a big responsibility here.

Emma Mack, *store owner*

I've lived in this town for more than 50 years. I own a small shop on main street. My shop has changed but it's never grown any bigger since I've owned it. People visit from all over the world and they love to buy my souvenirs. I have a world map where visitors can put a pin to show where they live. I love my job and meeting new people. I try to help people from other countries remember Canada as a wonderful country.

I hope to retire but my three sons would like to keep the family business. We will need to expand the shop if it is going to support three families. The shop is always so crowded, we know that we would have enough customers to make our plan work. We want to expand into the empty lot just behind our current location. All we have to do is add to the back of the store. But what if we aren't allowed to expand? Will we have to sell the shop? Will we have to look for other ways to make a living?

Michael MacDonald, *grade 6 student*

There are elk in town all the time. My dad said it's because the highways, the railway, and the people have used up most of the best animal feeding grounds. Elk are neat to see, but I think they are scary, too, especially in their mating season. I don't like to meet them, especially when I'm alone. Their antlers are huge! They could flip me like a pancake, if they wanted to.

Your Turn

1. What concern about Banff does each person express?

2. If you were responsible for making the decision about development in this community, how would you make sure everyone's voice was heard?

3. Can everyone's concerns be answered fairly?

4. How would you decide whose needs would be met?

Le Ha Do, *mayor*

You know, a lot of people think of this town as home. We grew up here and to us, it is much more than a vacation spot. If we want to be able to live here, we need to be able to work. It feels great to have been as successful as we are! That doesn't mean we don't care for the environmental needs. It means we feel a real sense of belonging and ownership. We have to preserve the environment while providing the development that will keep the town an exciting place to be—for us and for everyone who visits us. Some development just has to happen. The tough question is how to develop without affecting the park any more than necessary.

Sarah & Samuel Hyslop, *developers*

We own a construction company. This town has been our home for a long time. When we decided to move here, we studied the architecture and materials that would keep the "small village" look. We learned as much as we could about ways of building that would not affect the environment too much. If building stops in this community, we'll have to move. It seems a shame because this is such a wonderful community to live in. We have been happy in our work, helping visitors and residents enjoy this beautiful park.

Early Stories of a National Park

Native peoples travelled through the area near present-day Banff long before European explorers discovered it in the 1800s. The Kootenay, Shushwap, Blackfoot, Cree, and Stoney were familiar with the area. Although European explorers and missionaries had visited, it was not until 1858 that Sir James Hector of the Palliser Expedition reported the existence of something exciting and unusual— warm sulphur springs. (The Palliser Expedition was sent by the government to make maps and record information about the environment in western Canada.)

In 1871, when British Columbia became Canada's sixth province, the federal government promised to build a railway linking British Columbia with the other provinces. The descriptions provided by the Palliser Expedition were helpful in planning the route of the railway. When the railway was built, it passed near the sulphur springs that Sir James Hector had written about. The first tourists arrived with the regular train service which began in 1884. Sir William Van Horne, the man responsible for completing the railway, was one of the first tourists to visit the area. Word about the wonderful area spread. Prospectors and miners arrived, too, and a silver mine was developed nearby.

Many people who visited the area soon realized that the glaciers, animals, mountains, sulphur springs, and rich forests were special. They encouraged the government to protect this area so that it would not simply become a place for mines and businesses. On November 25, 1885, the federal government created Banff National Park. At this time, the park consisted of only the area surrounding the sulphur springs.

Slowly, Banff grew as a tourist area. The landscape was one attraction. The other was the springs, which some people believe can heal the sick. Dr. Robert G.

Tourism grew in Banff as a result of the sulphur springs. This photograph from about 1900 shows people enjoying the soothing, warm water.

Brett moved to the area and built a **sanitarium.** This sanitarium could house 50 tourists and 40 patients who wanted to bathe in the warm springs. Dr. Brett also opened a small souvenir shop and sold spring water in small bottles.

Because Banff was a national park, all rules and decisions about the area were made by the federal government in Ottawa, Ontario. By the early 1900s, Ottawa was looking to the future. The motor car was becoming more popular. The government worried that if motor cars were allowed in the park, the wild animals would be frightened away.

Concerns about motor cars came true in the summer of 1904. Even though there was no road from Calgary to Banff, adventurous tourists drove their motor cars along railway tracks into the park. When people in the federal government learned of this, they made a law to prevent cars from entering the park. People who broke the law could be fined $50 or sent to jail for three months.

In 1914, the federal government started letting cars into the park. Drivers, however, were not allowed to exceed a speed of 11 kilometres per hour.

Your Turn

1. Who do you think should make laws for communities like Banff? Why?

2. Why do you think the federal government decided to allow cars into the park in 1914?

3. How do you think traffic has affected Banff National Park?

4. Do you think the federal government should have allowed cars into the park? Explain your answer.

Hutterites are a group who share common religious beliefs and choose to live together in large farming colonies. These Hutterite women have just learned how to drive a truck.

The Hutterites:

Government in a Colony

Hutterites are a group of people who share common religious beliefs. Many Hutterites settled in Manitoba and Alberta when they first came to Canada. They choose to live together on large farms called colonies. Most colonies have 90 or 100 people. When a colony grows to about 125 people, the colony usually divides and another colony begins.

Hutterites believe that they must live by rules found in the Bible. All people of the colony must follow the teachings of Jesus Christ. Hutterites do not believe in private ownership. Everything they have is shared for the benefit of all the people in the colony.

Hutterite colonies have a three level form of local government:

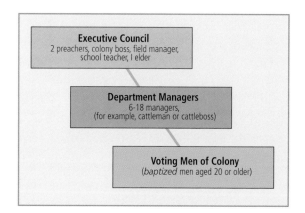

Executive Council
2 preachers, colony boss, field manager, school teacher, I elder

Department Managers
6-18 managers,
(for example, cattleman or cattleboss)

Voting Men of Colony
(*baptized* men aged 20 or older)

The Hutterite colony leader is the preacher. His role is to guide the life and work of the colony's people in a way that shows obedience to teachings of the Bible. A preacher is nominated from the voting men of the colony. The election of the preacher begins with a nomination of three candidates. To be nominated, a man must have at least five votes. The names of the candidates are placed in a hat. The person who has his name drawn out of the hat becomes the preacher. After a **probationary** period, the preacher is **ordained** for life.

The preacher is helped by an assistant preacher who is usually in charge of the German school. The preachers are part of the Executive Council. Other members of the Executive Council are chosen from the people of the colony. One of the most important elected positions is the "steward" or "householder" who is sometimes called the colony boss. The steward is chosen by a majority vote. He is in charge of caring for the colony's money and for the sale and purchase of goods. When large amounts of money are involved, the colony boss needs the approval of the Executive Council.

The field manager is an elected official who directs the farm work program and the colony workers. Other elected positions are the department managers. These managers include the cattleman, or "cattle boss," the chickenman, the shoemaker, the blacksmith, and the cabinet maker. In some colonies, the wife of the preacher is elected as head seamstress. The head seamstress helps the men buy fabrics for the colony.

Every colony has a set of **regulations** that the people are expected to follow. The Sunday evening meeting is the time when colony members must report if another colony member has not lived by the regulations. If this happens, the head preacher usually warns the person about his or her behaviour. If the person is not seen to be changing, the preacher and elders will decide on a punishment.

Important decisions about the colony require the consensus of the voting men. Every man must agree upon the decision before any action can be taken. Women and unbaptized men under the age of 20 do not have a voice in government. Colony members without a voice do not vote on electing leaders or on colony business.

Your Turn

1. How is local government in a Hutterite colony similar to and different from the local government in your community? If you live in a Hutterite colony, compare your local government to that of another community in this chapter.

2. The voting men in the Hutterite colony make decisions by consensus. List and describe the other communities you have already learned about that work by consensus.

Salt Spring:
Government on an Island

The province of British Columbia is made up of the mainland and the large island known as Vancouver Island. It also includes a number of tiny islands located between the mainland and Vancouver Island. These islands are known as the Gulf Islands. Salt Spring Island is one of the Gulf Islands.

In winter, the population of Salt Spring Island is about 9000 people. Some of these people live in the village of Ganges; others live on land located throughout the island. The small harbour at Ganges is a busy place as sailboats and private yachts travel through

The harbours on Salt Spring Island are busy with yachts and sailboats. Many people would like to live on this island.

the islands. Two other island harbours receive ferries from Vancouver, Victoria, and Crofton. The ferries bring visitors travelling by car, bicycle, motor home, or on foot. Other visitors arrive by small sea planes. Many people would like to move to this beautiful island community.

Salt Spring Island is mostly forests and farm lands. Many years ago, the government of British Columbia decided that special care had to be taken to protect the environment of the Gulf Islands. The provincial government formed the Islands Trust Region. Its purpose is to preserve and protect the islands in as natural a state as possible.

The Islands Trust Region consists of fourteen Trust Committee Areas. Each area elects two trustees to do the work of the Islands Trust Region.

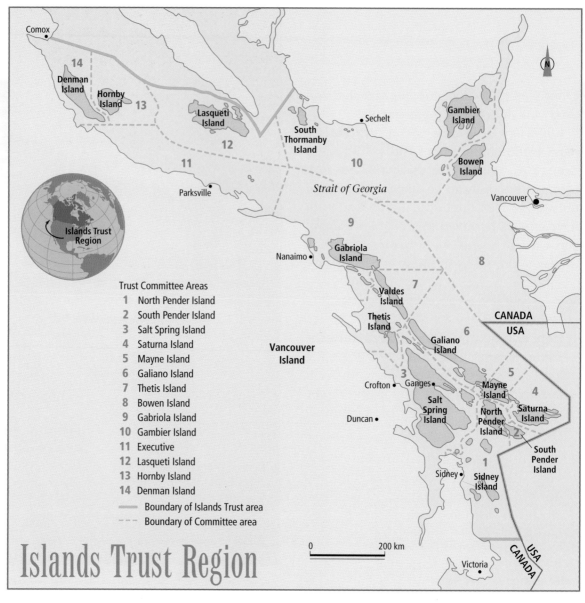

Trust Committee Areas
1 North Pender Island
2 South Pender Island
3 Salt Spring Island
4 Saturna Island
5 Mayne Island
6 Galiano Island
7 Thetis Island
8 Bowen Island
9 Gabriola Island
10 Gambier Island
11 Executive
12 Lasqueti Island
13 Hornby Island
14 Denman Island
——— Boundary of Islands Trust area
- - - - Boundary of Committee area

0   200 km

Islands Trust Region

Every three years, elections are held on Salt Spring Island. Instead of electing a mayor and council, voters elect people for two different forms of local government. One form of government is the Islands Trust Region. The people elect two trustees to carry out the work of the Islands Trust Region. One important part of the trustees' work is to make decisions about how land can be used.

The other form of government is called the Capital Regional District. This is local government for people who live on the Gulf Islands and on part of Vancouver Island. The people of Salt Spring Island elect one person to serve as director. There are six other districts, so six other directors are elected.

Each director works with his or her own community to identify services the community needs. Then they meet with the other directors to discuss how these needs might be met. One issue they might discuss is whether to encourage new businesses to come to their communities.

In 1999, the new territory of Nunavut will be created in response to the concerns of the Inuit of the eastern Arctic. They felt that the territorial government in Yellowknife was too far away to understand their needs.

Your Turn

The Island trustees and the director of the electoral district do not act as one council. They represent two different levels of government.

1. What do you think would happen if the two groups disagreed?

2. What could they do to build trust and communication?

3. What do you think might be the advantages and disadvantages of having two separate groups of elected people working for a community?

Native Peoples:
Self-Government

When Canada became a country in 1867, the constitution stated that the federal government was responsible for governing Native peoples and land reserved for them. In 1876, the Indian Act was passed. This Act listed responsibilities and agreements between the government and Native peoples. There are many problems with this Act. For example, it made rules about who would be considered a "**status**" or "Treaty" person, and who would not. If a Native woman married a Non-Native man, she lost her treaty status and the rights that went with it. This meant she was no longer considered a Treaty person by the federal government. Some Treaty men who fought for Canada in wars also lost their status, because they were away from their reserve for a long time. Through the passing years, Native peoples have grown unhappy with the way they are being governed. They do not believe their needs are being met by the federal government.

Native peoples do not wish to lose their cultural heritage. Native customs and traditions are connected to living in harmony with nature. These are different from the cultural heritage of many other Canadians. Many Native peoples feel that they need their own forms of local government.

The Native peoples of Canada are exploring different ways of forming government. The Inuit of the eastern Arctic are exploring a territorial form of government in the creation of Nunavut. You read about Nunavut in Chapter 2.

Today, some Native peoples live on reserves. There are more than 2000 reserves in Canada. On most reserves, you will find a band council, consisting of an elected chief and councillors. The Indian Act states that a council may have only one chief, who must be elected. A council may have between two and twelve councillors. There is to be 1 councillor for every 100 people living on the reserve. A band council may make laws that relate to the day-to-day life and business of the reserve such as housing, roads, and the protection of wildlife.

A large number of Native peoples, including Metis, live in cities, towns, villages, and hamlets across Canada. It is more difficult to keep Native cultural heritage alive in these larger communities.

On reserves and in other Canadian communities, Native peoples are working to find ways to govern themselves. There are four main goals Native peoples want in forming self-government.

1. To have more control over decision-making about Native local community issues.

2. To preserve the cultural identity of Native peoples, wherever they live in Canada.

3. To increase the **awareness** of Non-Native people about the unique needs of Native peoples.

4. To have greater responsibility for traditional ways of life, including fishing and hunting rights, education, and law enforcement.

Your Turn

Today, Native peoples in urban communities have begun to provide services to each other. One example is the establishment of Native Friendship Centres. Find out the purpose of a Native Friendship Centre.

Ideas for Using Information:

Forming and Considering Opinions

To form a responsible opinion, try the following:

1. define the issue

2. gather information
   ➤ what are the differing points of view?
   ➤ are there special considerations, such as laws?
   ➤ clarify what information is factual and what is point-of-view or opinion

3. try to understand the viewpoints
   ➤ determine the arguments for and against each viewpoint
   ➤ examine your own beliefs

When expressing an opinion, remember the following:

1. include your reasons

2. listen to others

When considering another person's opinion, try the following:

1. show respect for everyone's right to have differing opinions by being a good listener

2. avoid becoming angry if others don't agree with you

3. determine the similarities and differences between opinions

4. try to see what factors have caused the other person to form a different opinion

5. be willing to learn new information and reconsider your position

Test it out...

Imagine a situation in a community where everyone is talking about pollution in a lake. Cleaning up the pollution will cost money. Closing the factory that is causing the pollution will cost jobs. Consider the viewpoints of the fishers, citizens whose water comes from the lake, the factory owners, environmentalists, and elected leaders.

Chapter 7

Citizen's Voice

Chapter Focus

Many factors influence the way our representatives in government make decisions. When making decisions, they ask themselves many questions, such as: Is this decision for the good of the people? If this decision is not the best one, is it the only one that can be reached? What will the people think about this decision?

People can express their opinions in many different ways. This chapter will examine a number of ways you can have a voice in influencing decisions that are being made by government leaders.

As you read this chapter, consider these questions:

If a leader makes an unpopular decision, how can we let him or her know?

➤ How can people who are too young to vote influence the government?

➤ How do governments know what is the best decision?

➤ How does a government decide whose needs will be met?

➤ What is public opinion?

➤ How do we keep government responsible?

➤ What is lobbying?

Individual Power

There are many ways that people can express their wishes and share their ideas with politicians. There are some ways of expressing opinions that can be done by one person. This is "individual voice." One of the important ways you can express your individual voice is by voting at election time. When you vote, you are helping choose the kind of people and ideas that will be working for you.

Your personal power can also be expressed by contributing your voice to a group. "Group voice" can be an effective way to influence government leaders. There are a number of ways to participate in group voice. A **lobby group** brings people together to use their group voice. A **petition** allows people to use their group voice even without meeting together.

Vocabulary

acclamation —*n.* election without opposition; a public office won because there was no competition

advocacy —*n.* active support of an idea, cause, or policy, such as rights for people with disabilities

affirming —*v.* showing or demonstrating support

agenda —*n.* a list of things to be discussed

ballot —*n.* the official piece of paper used in voting

crusade —*n.* a vigorous movement for a cause

enumeration list —*n.* official list of eligible voters

enumerators —*n.* people who compile lists of eligible voters

exploitation —*n.* the act of using other people for selfish reasons

immigrant —*n.* a person who has come to a new country to live

lobby group —*n.* a group of people who try to influence political decisions

petition —*n.* a formal request to government which has been signed by many people

town hall meeting —*n.* an open meeting of citizens in which government representatives give information and citizens voice their ideas and opinions

Craig Kielburger formed a youth organization called "Free the Children" to raise money to publicize the facts about child labour.

Profile: Craig Kielburger
A Young Voice

This profile is about a young person who wanted to make a difference for other young people in the world. Although he is too young to vote, he is using his voice to influence others.

Craig Kielburger is a teenaged student from Toronto. Craig became concerned when he learned that in some parts of the world, very young children must go to work. He learned more than two hundred million children under the age of 14 are working full time throughout the world.

One country Craig learned about was India. He discovered that in parts of India there are children who work up to 80 hours a week making bricks and weaving carpets. The government of India has laws against child labour, but the laws are not being enforced. Craig believed he could help by using his citizen's voice. He formed a youth organization called "Free the Children." The purpose of his organization is to raise money to publicize the facts about child labour.

In 1996, Craig travelled to New Delhi, India to speak against the **exploitation** of children. At the same time, Canadian prime minister Jean Chretien was in New Delhi discussing trade issues with India's leaders. Craig managed to introduce two young Indian children to reporters. Both children told stories of beatings during their years as carpet weavers. The prime minister heard about Craig's **crusade** against child labour. He agreed to meet with Craig. At their meeting, Craig encouraged the prime minister to think about child labour before agreeing to trade with a country.

Craig Kielburger's experiences show that all people can have their voice heard. Craig has earned the respect of citizens and world leaders.

Your Turn

1. Craig has earned respect from adults and children throughout Canada. How has he done this?

2. Is there an issue in your family, your school, or your community in which you want to have a voice? Use Craig's example and the ideas in this chapter to establish a plan to express your voice.

Individual Power:

Letters to the Editor

The editorial section of the newspaper is where the editor of the paper states his or her views about a current issue. The editorial section in newspapers is widely read in Canada. Magazines also print letters to the editor. All citizens have the right to send a letter to the editor expressing their point-of-view. For every issue of the paper or magazine, the editor selects and prints a number of the letters.

Letters to the editor give people an opportunity to say what is on their mind. The following two letters about a proposal to build a new shopping centre were sent to a newspaper editor. Editors like to publish letters that speak about a current issue that is of interest to the public. If you were the editor, which letter would you publish? Why?

Letters to the editor may be in favour of an issue or they may be against an issue. A letter can also raise an issue by asking questions about

Dear Editor:

Yesterday I read about the proposal to build another shopping centre in our community. This plan concerns me. The developers want to put the shopping centre right across the street from the school. There is a lot of traffic coming in and out of a shopping centre. This won't be very safe for the children.

This is also not a good move for business. I have two friends who have gone out of business this year. There were just too many businesses trying to serve the same need. This town is barely able to support the businesses we already have. It doesn't make sense to open more shopping space.

Sincerely,

Susan MacAlister

Dear Editor:

I am writing about the new shopping centre that is planned in my community. I think it is a really poor idea to build another shopping centre. It's just dumb, dumb, *dumb!* What were these people thinking? They need to open their eyes. We don't want any more shopping centres.

anonymous

something which is of concern. Some people offer their solutions to a problem. Whatever the purpose, a good letter to the editor follows some rules:

1. Letters should include the name, telephone number, and address of the writer. This shows the editor that you are willing to take responsibility for your own opinion. Editors will not print letters unless they know the identity of the writer. (You can ask that it be printed anonymously, but you cannot be anonymous to the editor.)
2. Letters should be short and clearly express your point-of-view.
3. Letters should focus on ideas rather than emotions.
4. Opinions need to be explained.

Individual Power:
Contacting Your Representative

All elected representatives keep an office and are available by phone, mail, and often by Email and fax. Elected representatives have a responsibility to listen to the concerns of people in their constituency. Letters to Members of Parliament do not require postage.

When you are contacting a representative, it is helpful to follow some simple rules:

1. Contact your representative when the issue is current.
2. Always identify yourself.
3. Be prepared to state clearly why you are making contact. What is the issue? Tell how the issue affects you, your family, your business, or your community.
4. Use only known facts or first hand knowledge.
5. Describe a preferred solution if you have one.
6. Speak calmly and politely.

You can contact your representative by phone, mail, Email, or fax.

Individual Power:
Participating in Local Government Council Meetings

Most meetings of city or town councils are open to the public. It is a good idea to begin by contacting your representative in local government. He or she will be able to tell you how the meetings work. It is also helpful to know what is on the meeting **agenda** on the day you plan to attend.

Although citizens may attend a council meeting, they may speak only if they are part of the agenda. To be included on the agenda of a council meeting, a person should begin by contacting the mayor, chief, reeve, or a member of council. They will help you by

This photograph shows Canadian broadcaster Peter Mansbridge conducting a town hall meeting with Prime Minister Jean Chretien. The meeting took place at Ottawa University in 1996. Ordinary citizens were invited to ask questions and express their opinions about current issues.

explaining how to be included on the agenda of your community council.

Another place to express your opinion to your representatives is at a **town hall meeting**. This kind of meeting is called during election campaigns, or when an important decision must be made. In most town hall meetings, the representatives give information about their plans and invite comments from the citizens in attendance.

What Is Public Opinion?

There are times when people choose to work together to be sure their voice is heard. When a large number of people express the same thoughts, it is called public opinion. Public opinion is very important to government representatives. It tells them what the people want done about an issue.

Some people make it their job to collect and publish public opinion. These people are called pollsters. You may have heard of Angus Reid polls or Gallup polls. Both pollsters use questionnaires to collect and measure public opinion. The Angus Reid Group asks Canadians

SIXTY PER CENT OF CANADIANS SAY NO TO HIGHER TAXES

POLL SHOWS THAT ONE-FIFTH OF CANADIANS ARE UNDECIDED ABOUT EDUCATION CUTS

Fifty Per Cent of Voters Believe Government Is Overspending

about 50 000 questions each year. This polling company is hired to find out all kinds of things about how Canadians think, how they vote, what products they buy, what government services they value, and what issues concern them.

Very few citizens are actually contacted when a poll is taken. Pollsters have mathematical formulas that help them know how many people must participate in a poll for the information to be fairly accurate. Fewer than 2000 Canadians provide a national sample.

Polls may influence the way elected representatives work. At election time, polls are often used to identify the issues people are most interested in. Some voters are also influenced by polls showing which candidate in an election is most popular.

Your Turn

1. How do you think the information given in the newspaper headings on the previous page was gathered?

2. Who do you think would hire pollsters?

3. Why do you think the government would want to know what government services Canadians value most?

4. If your school were a town, and you were the mayor, what questions would you ask in a poll of the citizens?

5. Try testing one question in a public opinion poll in your class. Identify an issue like, "Should snowballs be allowed on the school ground?" Don't discuss what you think with anyone. Distribute small pieces of paper to the class and ask them to answer the question using "yes" or "no." Record all the responses on a class list. Next, tally the opinions of every fourth person on the class list. Using mathematical rate pairs, compare the results of the opinion poll and the total class. Did you find a similar pattern?

6. At election time, how do you think polls might influence voters?

How Does the Election Process Work?

The purpose of an election is to choose people who will represent our opinions and carry on the business of government in ways that are responsible. A candidate is elected to represent the people in a specific area. In federal and provincial elections, this area is called a

Enumerators go door-to-door to gather information about eligible voters.

riding or a constituency. Both words mean the same thing. In a municipal election the area in a city is called a ward. These divisions are created to make sure that the people of the community have fair representation in government. The process of organizing for an election is similar at all levels of government.

Federal and provincial elections take place at least every five years. In towns and cities, local government elections take place every three years. Local elections can also be called civic or municipal elections.

Preparing for a Local Election

Local elections are held every three years. In each community, one civic official is appointed to the job of returning officer. The returning officer must prepare a list of all the people who are eligible to vote. This is an important job. A returning officer may prepare the voting

This billboard shows the prime minister and a local candidate from his party. What is the purpose of political posters like this one?

list in one of two ways. She or he may use the National Register of Electors, or may hire people in the community to do the job.

In 1997, the federal government prepared a National Register of Electors. This is a computer list of all eligible voters. Local communities may use the National Register to identify the list of eligible voters in an area. In some areas of the country, the returning officer may choose to hire a number of **enumerators** to go door-to-door to collect the names of eligible voters.

The returning officer must identify places, called polling stations, where the voting will take place. Schools and community centres are often used as polling stations. Another responsibility of a returning officer is to make sure that enough **ballots** are printed for all the people who are eligible to vote. It is the job of the returning officer to see that all goes smoothly on election day, and that election laws are not broken.

Running for Office

At the local level, eligible candidates put their names forward to run for elected office. This must be done on nomination day, which is four weeks before election day. A person must possess certain qualifications to be eligible to become a candidate. Each province or territory will list the qualifications a person must meet to become a candidate for municipal or school board office.

The list below gives examples of the necessary qualifications.

A candidate must:
➤ be a Canadian citizen
➤ be at least 18 years old
➤ have lived in the community for a minimum of six months before nomination day
➤ have between 5 and 25 eligible voters sign the "Nomination for Office" papers
➤ pay $100 as a deposit

This photograph shows leaders of three different political parties debating issues before the provincial election in Alberta in 1997. What is the purpose of political debates?

> deliver nomination papers and deposit fee to the local government office by noon on nomination day

Campaigning

In the weeks leading to election day, candidates are busy campaigning. They speak about the issues in the community and hope to convince people to vote for them.

Candidates use many methods to try to get their message to the voters. Posters and signs are placed in areas of the community where they can be easily seen. These have the candidate's name printed in large letters to help people remember the candidate's name. Sometimes the candidate's picture is on the posters and signs. There may be a slogan, too.

Candidates also speak at public meetings and in the media. Some appear on television and debate public issues with other candidates. Most candidates go from door-to-door to meet people and answer questions. Sometimes volunteers also campaign door-to-door for their candidate. They answer questions about the plans of the candidate they are helping and deliver information brochures to people. In all these ways candidates try to inform voters about their particular platform.

During election time, it is a good idea to know what questions you would like answered by a candidate who knocks on your door.

When there is only one candidate for a position of office, that candidate is declared elected by **acclamation.** When this happens, the candidate does not have to campaign during the election period.

Who Is Eligible to Vote?

In a municipal election, a person is able to vote if they:
> are Canadian citizens
> are the age of majority (usually 18 years old)
> have lived in the community for at least six months before election day

Preparing to Cast a Responsible Vote

Once an election has been called, eligible voters have two very important tasks.

The first task is to be informed about when and where to vote. Eligible voters need to check the **enumeration list** to be sure that their name has been included.

The second important job of eligible voters is to become informed about the issues and

All voters have the responsibility of informing themselves so that they can make wise decisions.

the candidates. In an election there may be one or more main issues in a community. One issue might be about whether or not to build a special community facility like a stadium. Another might be about whether taxes are fair for the services offered.

A responsible voter needs to listen to many different viewpoints. During an election, listening will help a person learn about problems and begin to make a decision about what would be best for the community. Once a voter understands the issues, it becomes easier to choose the candidate who will do the best job.

Voters can become informed in many ways. Newspapers, television, radio, town hall meetings, and debates are all helpful. Talking to people in the community, to candidates, and their campaign teams can also be a source of information. There are times when it will be important to do some research. A responsible decision is made with facts as well as opinions.

On Election Day

On election day, eligible voters go to their polling stations. There are times when it is difficult for a person to vote at the community polling station. A voter might be ill in a hospital or away on business or vacation. Communities make arrangements for special polling stations in hospitals and nursing homes. When people will be away on voting day, they may vote at advance polls held from 5 to 11 days before election day.

Voting begins at 9:00 AM and ends at 8:00 PM. There can be no campaigning on election day. This is the day for a voter to make final decisions based upon what they have learned during the campaign.

At the polling station, a voter goes to a table where the voter list is kept. The voter's name will be crossed off the list by a poll clerk. This is so that a voter may not vote more than once during an election. A deputy returning officer gives a ballot to the voter. The candidate's names are listed on the ballot.

After the voter has been given a ballot, he or she goes to a polling booth. This is usually a small counter with sides so that no one can see how a person votes. In Canada, ballots are marked with an X. Voters need to read the instructions on the ballot. Ballots that are marked incorrectly are called spoiled ballots. If a ballot is spoiled, it will not be counted.

When the voter has marked the ballot, he or she takes it to the deputy returning officer who puts the ballot in the ballot box. This ballot box is kept locked until the polling station closes at 8:00 PM. After the polling station closes, the ballot boxes are opened and the ballots are counted.

This voter is putting an **X** on her ballot, beside her candidate of choice.

A Right and Responsibility

Participating in the election process is a very important way of using your voice. In Canada and other democratic countries, using your voice to vote is a right. In some countries, citizens do not have the right to vote for their leaders. Voting is also a responsibility. Voting is the best way citizens have to make sure that government leaders are wise and trustworthy people.

In Canada, there is a problem. Many people do not accept their right and responsibility to vote. Reasons why some people do not vote include:

1. They think that their vote will not make any difference to the election outcome.

2. They do not like any of the candidates or platforms.

3. They have not informed themselves about the candidates and the issues, and so they do not know who to vote for.

Your Turn

1. Why do you think people do not vote?

2. Find out the voter turn-out in your last local election.

3. What might happen to communities where people do not vote?

4. What do you think could or should be done to encourage more people to vote?

Becoming a Canadian Citizen

In order to vote in an election, or to hold a government office, a person must be a Canadian citizen. Citizenship means being counted. Anyone born in Canada is automatically a Canadian citizen. Anyone born outside of Canada who has a Canadian parent is also automatically a Canadian citizen.

In Canada there are many people who have moved here from countries all around the world. When a person moves from one country to another, the person is known as an **immigrant.** Some immigrants live and work in Canada, but do not choose to become Canadian citizens. Many other immigrants want to make Canada their home. They also want to have a voice in the governing of Canada. To do this, a person must become a Canadian citizen.

To live in Canada, an immigrant must have the permission of the federal government. This permission is called landed immigrant status. A landed immigrant must live in Canada at least three years before applying for citizenship. After this time, a landed immigrant may take a citizenship test. This test has questions about the history of

These people have passed the Canadian citizenship test and are swearing the oath of citizenship.

Canada, current information about Canada, and some questions about the province or territory in which the person lives. After an immigrant has passed the test, he or she is invited to a citizenship court. There, a special ceremony is held and the person repeats the "Oath of Citizenship" to a judge.

The Oath of Citizenship

I, _____ , swear (or affirm) that I will be faithful and bear allegiance to Her Majesty Queen Elizabeth the Second, Queen of Canada, her Heirs and Successors, according to law and that I will faithfully observe the laws of Canada and fulfill my duties as a Canadian Citizen.

Lobby Groups:
Working with Others to Influence Government

Making decisions on behalf of other people is a difficult job. Our representatives are expected to work in the best interests of the community. This does not mean that all decisions will satisfy or meet the needs of all the people. Citizens can work with elected representatives to share different points-of-view and to share information that will lead to the best decision for the most people.

Citizens acting as a group to make their concerns known are called lobby groups or special interest groups. Their purpose is to influence government as it does the work of making laws and of providing services.

Lobbying is done in many different ways. Contributing time, money, or skills to a political campaign is one form of lobbying. This is because you are supporting the beliefs of a group that you hope will become the government leaders. Groups of people who have similar needs can join together to help each other. These groups may be called a council, a league, a chamber, a union, an association, or a foundation.

The Chamber of Commerce is an example of a business group that meets to discuss the unique needs of business owners. Often a branch of the Chamber of Commerce will need the support of local government if they are to be successful in running their businesses. Sunday shopping is a local government decision that affects businesses.

The Canadian Paraplegic Association (CPA) is a national organization that encourages the independence and full participation of Canadians with spinal cord injuries or other conditions that limit their ability to move. The purpose of the CPA is to support the needs and rights of people with disabilities through education, counselling, and **advocacy**. The association recommends changes to policies and attitudes so that people with disabilities can lead fulfilling lives. For example, the CPA helped set guidelines for making facilities, exhibits, and programs at Canada's national parks easy for people with disabilities to use.

Lobbying can be done in many ways. Some groups meet with government representatives. Some groups organize petitions to send to government representatives.

Listed below are seven guidelines to organize an effective lobby:

1. Know how decisions are made at the level of government you plan to lobby.

2. Know the legal ways to lobby.

3. Know exactly what you want changed and how this change will be in the best interests of the public.

4. Know which other groups share an interest in the same issue. Find out what they know and how they are working to influence government.

5. Have accurate information supported by well-known facts.

6. Have an action plan including what jobs to do, how to do them, who is to do them, and when they are to be finished.

7. Be honest.

Lobbying:
Petitions and Plebiscites

Petitions are one way that many citizens can join together and become more directly involved in influencing government. Petitions can be presented to all levels of government.

There are a number of guidelines for writing and filing a petition:

1. Learn as much as you can about the problem or change that you would like to see. Be sure that you are approaching the level of government that has the power to do what you are asking.

2. Write the purpose of your petition in a clear sentence so that people who read the petition will understand your objective. The purpose statement must be written clearly at the top of every page of the petition.

3. Organize each petition page so that people who agree with your viewpoint can sign it. There must be spaces for each person's signature, printed name, address, and the date.

These men are holding a petition that was signed by 1100 concerned citizens. The goal of this petition was to have Video Lottery Terminals (VLTs) removed from the town of Rocky Mountain House, Alberta.

4. Locate public places where you can leave the petition for other people to see. You might also want to give copies of the petition to other supporters who will help gather signatures.

5. In municipal politics, signatures on an official petition can be gathered for 60 days only. After this time, the petition must be filed with the government office if it is to be valid. In order for a government to consider a change, a petition must be signed by enough eligible voters to equal 10 per cent of the people living in the riding or constituency.

Some petitions ask for a special vote of all the eligible voters in the community. This special vote is called a plebiscite. In Chapter 2, you read about a plebiscite in the Arctic. A plebiscite allows eligible citizens to have a direct say on a local issue. When at least five per cent of the people in communities of more than 1000 people sign a petition for a plebiscite, the local government must arrange the plebiscite. In communities of fewer than 1000 people, the petition must contain the signatures of at least 10 per cent of the people.

Your Turn

1. Why do you think that a smaller community needs a larger per cent of signatures on a petition before a plebiscite can be called?

2. In Chapter 1, you read about government in ancient Greece. How do you think a plebiscite is similar to government in ancient Greece?

Lobbying:
Peaceful Demonstrations and Rallies

The Charter of Rights allows people to gather in large groups to demonstrate how they feel about issues. A peaceful demonstration usually involves a group of people walking through the streets. Sometimes it involves people riding tractors, bicycles, or boats. In order to have a peaceful demonstration, a group registers with the local government. The group will be asked the date, route, location, and reason for the demonstration. If the demonstration is thought to be safe and will not interfere with the rights of others, a permit is given. The demonstration ends with a rally.

These people attended a rally in Kitchener, Ontario in 1996 to voice their concern about labour practices.

Rallies are gatherings of people who want to encourage one another, express their concerns, and teach people about a particular issue. They are often held in stadiums, in front of government buildings, on logging roads, or in front of businesses. When people gather, they might listen to speeches and music, sing songs, and pray. They hope that others will listen and become interested, too.

Ideas for Applying Strategies:
Using Your Voice

As citizens, it is important to have ways to express our voice. We need to be able to express our concerns and wishes. Expressing your voice can also be for the purpose of **affirming** what is happening. Leaders and community members need to hear when we are pleased as well as when we are concerned. Affirming lets leaders know when decisions and actions should be continued.

In this chapter, you have been introduced to a number of strategies citizens can use to express wishes or opinions. Although some ways of expressing your voice, such as voting, cannot be used until you are older, others, such as letter writing, can be used immediately.

Throughout this text, you have been encouraged to be an informed citizen. Look carefully at what is happening in the communities where you have membership. These might include your school, your neighbourhood, or your city. Personal experiences are one source of information. Your school council and newsletter might be a source of information about your school community. Your local newspaper, television, and radio are sources of information about your municipality. Is there anything happening in your community right now that causes you concern? Are there things you are pleased about?

Your Turn

If you feel strongly about something happening around you, consider using your individual voice.

1. Gather and carefully examine information.

2. Examine points-of-view that are different from your own.

3. Make a plan by identifying your audience (who to tell), and your strategy (how to tell).

4. Before putting your plan into action, you might want to share it with an adult you trust.

5. Then, clearly state your point.

Chapter 8

Choosing Responsible Leaders

Chapter Focus

How do you learn about a candidate's position on election issues? It is important to have a good sense of how the person you elect thinks. During an election, candidates usually have signs and brochures. A brochure might feature a biography, statements about what the candidate believes about key election issues, and what she or he promises to do when elected. Some candidates will attend town hall meetings. Some will go on radio or television. Many campaign by going door-to-door.

In this chapter, you will have the opportunity to examine ways that voters can prepare to make informed and responsible decisions on election day.

As you read this chapter, consider these questions:

➤ What are the qualities of a good leader?

➤ Why is it important to have good leaders?

➤ What is negative campaigning?

➤ What types of power do leaders possess?

➤ How does debate contribute to democracy?

Vocabulary

code of conduct –*n.* a collection of rules or laws about how to behave

compensation –*n.* something given as repayment for a loss

conduct –*n.* behaviour or way of acting

enticed –*v.* tempted by being offered a reward

media –*n.* means of mass communication, such as radio, newspapers, television, billboards

negotiate –*v.* to try to reach an agreement through discussion

office –*n.* in politics, a political position, such as a city councillor

opponents –*n.* people with the opposite point-of-view

platforms –*n.* the promised action plans of political candidates

qualifications –*n.* the characteristics or skills that make a person suitable for a job

What Might You Expect from a Good Leader?

In Chapter 1, you learned about the feudal system of government in England. Knights existed during this time to protect feudal lords. In order to be a knight, a man had to swear to follow the rules of a **code of conduct**. In feudal times, this was called chivalry. The rules of chivalry were:

➤ defend the weak
➤ obey the king
➤ love the country
➤ obey the church
➤ never retreat in battle
➤ be unselfish
➤ tell the truth
➤ keep promises
➤ fight for right against evil.

Even though the feudal system ended long ago, the idea of a code of conduct continues to be used by many groups of people. For example, teachers have a Code of Ethics. A code of conduct can also be called an oath, a covenant, a pledge, or an agreement. For example, doctors have a code called the Hippocratic Oath.

This chapter is about choosing good leaders. As you read about the different people, think about what you would include in a code of conduct for community leaders.

Your Turn

1. Do you belong to any groups that have a code of conduct?

2. Does your school or class have a covenant?

3. Do leaders you know follow a good code of conduct?

Case Study:
Election Time in Oasis

This case study is about a fictitious community called Oasis. As you read about the different **platforms** of the candidates running in the local election, consider the following questions:

➤ What are the issues in the election?

➤ What are the qualities of the individual candidates?

➤ What are the **qualifications** of each candidate?

➤ What is the main issue in the election?

➤ What is each candidate's platform?

The people of the small town of Oasis are concerned. The old highway ran through the town, but the new highway has been built some distance away from the town. Now, travellers no longer stop in Oasis to buy gas, food, or stay at the motel. Local businesses have lost sales, and some have closed down. Some residents are talking seriously about moving away from Oasis. Something has to be done.

The townspeople are currently in the process of electing a new mayor. They have asked for a town hall meeting. They want to learn the names and platforms of each candidate. They also want to learn about the qualities and qualifications of each candidate.

Jane Powell is the **incumbent** mayor. She is 43 years old and has just finished a three-year term as the mayor of Oasis. Jane owns her own construction business and employs 25 Oasis residents. Jane is president of the local Sports Council. She volunteers much of her time ensuring that the teenagers of Oasis have a variety of sporting activities in which to participate. Jane believes that by making Oasis a safe and active place for young people, they will take pride in their community. This will result in reduced crime levels.

Jane often points out that since there is now less traffic in town, there have been far fewer traffic accidents. People do not have to worry nearly as much about crossing the main street and children are able to ride their bikes safely again.

Jane Powell said, "We don't have to use tricks to pull people into Oasis. We need to continue our good work in making Oasis a safe and attractive place to live. New residents will keep Oasis alive. Let's remember the name of our town. That tells what people around here really value. I've been a good mayor for the town. You know I work hard and I do what I say I'll do. You can count on me!"

Brian Fowler works for the local radio station. He is 45 years old. He hosts a phone-in talk show. Brian has lived in the town for 10 years. His two children attend Oasis Elementary School. Brian is also the choir director for the Oasis Warblers. Recently Brian coordinated a fund raiser that paid for three local high school students to attend university for a year.

Brian thinks that the provincial government should be providing **compensation** to Oasis, because it was a provincial government decision to build the new highway far away from Oasis.

Brian Fowler said, "To be a good politician, you have to be in touch with the people. You have to know what people are really thinking in order to do a good job of representing their interests. You cannot get much closer to the thoughts of the people than I do on my talk show. You know what I'm saying is true because many of you phone the show every week!

"My station manager has already agreed to let me use my talk show to help solve our crisis. I promise to work hard for our community."

Zinada Ladak has been a resident of Oasis for twenty years. She is 62 years old. She is a real estate agent and a member of the Oasis Chamber of Commerce.

Zinada thinks that the town's residents must work together to revive the economy of Oasis. Travellers need to be encouraged to come into Oasis. She proposes developing a tourist attraction that would bring people to the town.

Zinada Ladak said, "We have to be creative. Look at all of the small Canadian communities who have rebuilt their towns. Chemainus in British Columbia is called "the little town that did." It was a dying community but the people were creative. They painted wonderful murals that show the history of the town and Vancouver Island. Other towns have built water slides, gardens, and entertainment parks. There's no limit to the things we could do. Things are just getting worse while we sit around talking. We have to act quickly."

Simon Eaglefeather has lived in the town of Oasis for the last eight years. He is a 34-year-old lawyer.

Simon feels that the local and provincial government must make the town prosperous again without losing sight of the many other needs of the townspeople. He is committed to maintaining a rural community atmosphere.

Simon Eaglefeather said, "My legal background is going to be essential as we begin to work with our provincial government to make changes. I know this community. You know I care deeply about our quality of life. Many of you have used my services and you know I can be trusted. We have to move cautiously and consider all the factors. Rushing without thinking could create many new problems."

Your Turn

1. What qualifications will the new leader of Oasis require?

2. Which candidate do you think would be the best choice?

3. Which plan would work to restore the town?

Negative Campaigning

The election in Oasis has a fifth candidate. **Bill Banks** is 45 years old. Bill has many friends around the town. People know Bill cares about Oasis, but some have a problem with Bill's campaign. They think he is using a style of campaigning called "negative campaigning." Sometimes you will hear this called "mud slinging."

Bill Banks said, "I've really heard enough from the other candidates! Who are they trying to fool? Everybody knows this town is in trouble, and we know who caused this mess. It's time for some firm action, and I'm the guy to do that for you. Don't be tricked by nice promises or excuses. They just hide the real issues. Remember, one of our candidates has a lot to gain from winning this election and that won't be money in your pocket or mine! Vote for me and I'll fix things up in no time."

Your Turn

1. What would Bill do if he was elected mayor of Oasis?

2. What do you think about Bill Bank's campaign?

3. Would you vote for Bill? Why?

4. If you were his friend, how would you advise him?

Power

Often people who hold an **office** are said to be "in power" or powerful. The information below describes different kinds of individual power.

Political Power
➤ can come from being a member of a major political party

➤ can come from taking a popular stand on an important issue

Positional Power
➤ can come from having job experience

Personal Power
➤ can come from friends, acquaintances, or from people who know about your work

Your Turn

Look again at each candidate for the office of mayor in Oasis.

1. What kind of power does each candidate have?

2. Why is it important to understand the power a candidate has?

Word Origins

The word **candidate** comes from the Latin words *candidus* meaning "white" and the suffix *-atus* meaning the "wearing of something." A Roman *candidatus* was a man who wanted to be elected to office. A candidatus wore a bleached white robe called a *toga*. This was a symbol that his character was spotless so he could be trusted.

Profile:
Chief Crowfoot

In history, some leaders are remembered as examples of excellent leadership. One of these great leaders was Chief Crowfoot. Crowfoot was chief of the Blackfoot in the 1800s. This was a time of great trouble for the Blackfoot. The Prairies were changing. Farmers and ranchers were settling on lands that were home to Native peoples. Chief Crowfoot spent most of his life working for peace. His wise leadership helped his people survive times and conditions which would forever change their lifestyle.

As a young man, Crowfoot gained a reputation among the Blackfoot for being courageous and successful in battle. Crowfoot became chief at a time when the buffalo still ran in great herds and the western lands of Canada were open prairies.

During his years as chief, Crowfoot saw more and more immigrants from eastern Canada, the United States, and Europe arriving on the Prairies. These settlers moved onto traditional hunting grounds. Non-Native hunters slaughtered buffalo by the thousands, and left the meat to rot. Crowfoot's people were hungry. Some of the young Blackfoot wanted to go to war against the immigrants. The Blackfoot had realized that the ways of the immigrants would not be good for their people. Crowfoot, however, feared that if his people went to war for the land, too many would die.

Crowfoot decided the best he could do for his people was to **negotiate** agreements with the newcomers. One very famous agreement was Treaty Number Seven.

In 1877, the Blackfoot, Sarcee, and Stoney peoples gathered at Blackfoot Crossing for the negotiations with the representatives of the government of Canada. Along with Chief Crowfoot were Chief Red Crow of the Bloods,

Chief Eagle Tail of the Peigans, Chief Bearspaw of the Stonies, and Chief Bull Head of the Sarcees. (The Blackfoot people consisted of the Blood, Blackfoot, and Peigan. The Sarcee and the Stoney were two other Native peoples who also lived on the Prairies.)

Chief Crowfoot was well-known to the Native peoples. The people respected him and had confidence in his ability to make good decisions. On the fourth day of negotiations, Chief Crowfoot stood to speak to the people who had gathered at Blackfoot Crossing. As he paused, the nearly 5000 people in the valley became silent. He said,

"While I speak be kind and patient. I have to speak for my people who are numerous and rely upon me to follow the course which in the future will tend to their good. The plains are large and wide. We are the children of the plains. It is our home and the buffalo has been our food, always. I hope you will look upon the Blackfoot, Bloods, Peigans, and Sarcees as your children now and that you will be considerate and charitable to them. They all expect me to speak for them, and I trust the Great Spirit will put into their breasts to be good people, also into the minds of all men, women, and children of future generations. The advice given to me and my people has proven good. If the police had not come to this country, where would we all be by now? Bad men and whiskey were killing us so fast that very few of us would be alive today. The Mounted Police have protected us as the feathers of the bird protect it from the frosts of winter. I wish all my people good and trust that all our hearts will increase in goodness from this day forward. I am satisfied. I will sign the Treaty."

Treaty Number Seven was signed first by Chief Crowfoot.

Life on the Prairies forever changed after Treaty Number Seven was signed. Among other issues, this treaty made way for cattle ranching,

Crowfoot was chief of the Blackfoot in the 1800s. This photograph was taken of him in 1885.

homesteading, the railway, and settlements. It also took away the freedom of the Native peoples to travel, camp, and hunt the way they had for hundreds of years. The Blackfoot, Stoney, and Sarcee peoples moved to reserves.

Chief Crowfoot died in 1890 and was buried at Blackfoot Crossing, a place close to his heart. He has been called the "Chief of Chiefs." The bronze plaque on his grave reads, "Father of his People."

Your Turn

1. What kind of power do you think Chief Crowfoot had?

2. Even though Chief Crowfoot encouraged his people to make a decision that some did not like, he was considered a great leader. What qualities do you think Chief Crowfoot had that made him a great leader?

Ideas for Gathering and Communicating Information:

Hearing Other Opinions

Town hall meetings and the **media** are sources of information about election issues and the candidates' viewpoints. Listening to debates is another way to learn about candidates.

A debate is a formal discussion to present viewpoints in an organized manner. Because a debate requires speakers to take turns, a debate allows listeners to hear both sides of an argument. In Canada, debating is the way we listen to one another in local, provincial, territorial, and federal government.

A debate is a formal discussion about a resolution. There are three different types of resolutions. They are:

1. Policy Resolutions

➤ For example: Should there be sports in schools?

➤ Should the legal age for driving be lowered?

A policy resolution tries to answer a "should" question. Debaters use a policy resolution when they are exploring what action should be taken on an issue.

2. Value Resolutions

➤ For example: A person must always be honest.

A value resolution tries to determine how people should "be" in our society. In an election, debaters use value resolutions to explore and state how they will behave once elected.

3. Fact Resolutions

➤ For example: Canada needs more jobs for people.

In an election campaign, debates on fact resolutions assist voters discover what candidates value.

Preparing for a Debate

1. Decide on the topic for discussion.
2. Decide the purpose of the discussion and the type of resolution that needs to be used.
3. Prepare a resolution question or statement.
4. Be clear about whether you will agree or disagree with the resolution.
5. Make a list of the reasons that support your point-of-view.
6. Take time to think about points that your **opponents** might make. Are there arguments you will be able to use to disprove opposing arguments?

Begin here
The resolution is read.

⬇

Next, the speaker "for" the resolution makes a short three minute speech. He or she talks about why the resolution is important. Usually this includes a description of the problems with the way things are now and evidence to prove that a problem exists. Once this has been done, the speaker introduces a plan that will improve the situation.

The speaker "for" the resolution now has two minutes to tell the audience why his or her opponent's point is wrong. The speaker does this by discussing a point made by the opposing speaker and showing exactly what is the problem with the point.

The speaker "for" the resolution now has two minutes to try to convince the audience to agree with her or his resolution and plan.

Conducting a Debate

A debate is organized so that the speakers take turns. The sample chart below will help you conduct a simple debate of your own.

When we understand debating, and practise it as students, we are learning a skill for life. Debating will help us be more effective citizens, by helping us think issues through. It will help us to participate better in meetings such as student council, community leagues, and other groups to which we belong. Many schools and universities have debating clubs. These clubs help people practise their skills. They are also fun for the participants and the audience.

As well as learning debating skills for our own use, we can better understand and appreciate debates in our communities and legislatures. Debates help us to evaluate our leaders and help us decide what might be best for our communities.

Your Turn

Try conducting a debate in your class. Use an issue from this book that interests you, or identify an issue in your school or community that you would like to learn more about.

A Simple Debate Structure

The speaker "against" the resolution also has three minutes to speak. It is the job of the opposing speaker to describe why the resolution is a poor idea. This person shows why the arguments made by the first speaker will not work.

The speaker "against" the resolution now has two minutes to tell the audience again why the "for" speaker's point is wrong. This is done by discussing a point made by the opposing speaker and showing exactly what is the problem with the point.

The speaker "against" the resolution now has two minutes to try to convince the audience to disagree with the first speaker's resolution and plan.

Conclusion

The responsible citizen of the future will stay informed about issues affecting life in her or his community. As we see our world become increasingly interconnected, many of these issues may also affect the global community. For example, a successful recycling program in your community may inspire other communities around the world to follow the same program.

The Future

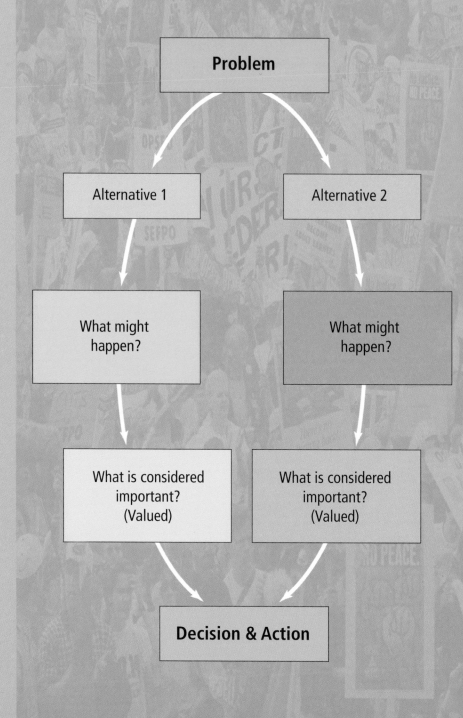

One way to become an involved citizen is to become a "community watcher." Newspapers, radio, television, magazines, and the Internet are all sources of information about issues in your community. Can you think of other sources?

In this text you have explored ways to use your voice to improve life in your community. You have the *right* to express your opinion and the *responsibility* to contribute to improving life in your community.

Local governments help us with the work of improving our communities. Many communities employ public planners. Public planners often begin their work by learning about the past. Events in a community's history can give clues about what will or will not work in the community in the future.

Planning for the future of a community takes careful work. Planning helps us move from how we are to how we want to be. People who plan communities must consider many factors. They must think about housing, education, transportation, needs of people with disabilities, recreation, safety, business, and industry. Planners also must think carefully about how the plans will affect the environment.

Your Turn

1. In pairs or groups of three, try being community planners. Design a landscape on a large piece of paper. Use a scale of 10 centimetres to equal 2 kilometres. Include a river or some other natural feature you might expect to see in a place where people would want to build a community.

2. Next, design a community on your landscape. Make movable pieces for buildings and use strips of paper for roads. Be creative. Try to think like a planner.

3. As you are working, keep a list of the changes you made, and the reason you made them.

4. Share your work with your class.

Planners study communities other than their own. They learn about problems facing other communities. They study solutions to these problems, and learn from the experience of others. Planners consider issues such as:
➤ air, water, and soil pollution
➤ diminishing natural resources
➤ species extinction
➤ technological changes
➤ social problems such as:
  ➤ unemployment
  ➤ crime
  ➤ drug and alcohol abuse
  ➤ hunger and poverty

Planners consider alternatives. A decision chart is one way of considering alternatives. Choose one of the issues on the above list. Look at the community you designed. Use a decision chart, like the one on the previous page, to develop a plan for preventing this issue from becoming a problem in your community.

Your Turn

In Chapter 8 you learned about codes of conduct. Take time now to make a personal code as a citizen. Are there choices you can make in your life that will help to solve or prevent problems? Include these ways in your personal code.

Find your voice. The future is just beginning.
You can be a part of influencing what happens.

—*Lynn A.A. Flaig and Kathryn E. Galvin*

Bibliography

Ardiel, William. *Structures of Canadian Municipal Organization* (discussion paper), 1990.

Barnett, Don C. and Lowry R. Knight. *The Hutterite People: A Religious Community.* Saskatoon: Western Extension College Educational Press, 1977.

Brown, Ron. *Ghost Towns of Canada.* Toronto: Cannonbooks, 1987.

Bunting, Trudi and Pierre Filion (eds). *Canadian Cities in Transition.* Toronto: Oxford University Press, 1991.

Canada Year Book 1997. Altona: Minister Responsible for Statistics Canada, 1996.

Canada's North: The Reference Manual. Ottawa: Canadian Government Publishing Centre, 1985.

Canadian Citizenship Education and Participation Study Guide. Calgary: Immigrant Aid Society, 1994.

Cotterell, Arthur (ed). *The Penguin Encyclopedia of Ancient Civilizations.* London: Rainbird, 1980.

Crick, Bernard. *Basic Forms of Government: A Sketch and a Model.* London: Macmillan, 1973.

Downs, Art (ed). *Banff: Park of All Seasons.* Surrey: Frontier Books, 1968.

FitzGerald, Patrick C. *Ancient China.* Oxford: Elsevier-Phaidon, 1978.

Flint, David. *The Hutterites: A Study in Prejudice.* Toronto: Oxford University Press, 1975.

Franz, Michael. *China Through the Ages: History of a Civilization.* Boulder: Westview Press, 1986.

Frideres, James S. *Native Peoples in Canada: Contemporary Conflicts.* Scarborough: Prentice-Hall, 1993.

Hibbert, Christopher. *The Story of England.* London: Phaidon, 1992.

Hosteller, John A. *Hutterite Life.* Kitchener: Herald Press, 1983.

Hunter, Diane et al (compilers). *The Lobbying Book: A Political Skills Group.* Winning Women: Calgary, 1990.

Krause, Robert M. and R.H. Wagenberg. *Introductory Readings in Canadian Government and Politics.* Toronto: Copp Clark Pitman, 1991.

Kurian, George T. *World Encyclopedia of Cities Vol. II, North America.* Santa Barbara: ABC - CLIO, 1994.

Law, Barbara (ed). *1996 Corpus Almanac and Canadian Sourcebook.* Don Mills: Mary Mancini, 1995.

Lustinger-Thaler, Henri (ed). *Political Arrangements: Power and the City.* Montreal: Black Rose Books, 1992.

Masson, Jack with Edward C. LeSage Jr. *Alberta's Local Governments: Politics and Democracy.* Edmonton: University of Alberta Press, 1994.

McTeer, Maureen. *Parliament: Canada's Democracy and How It Works.* Toronto: Random House of Canada, 1995.

Morton, Desmond. *Confederation: A Short History of Canada's Constitution.* Toronto: Umbrella Press, 1992.

Muligan, R.G. *Aristotle's Political Theory.* Oxford: Clarendon Press, 1977.

Nardo, Don. *Democracy.* San Diego: Lucent Books, 1994.

Peter, Karl A. *The Dynamics of Hutterite Society: An Analytical Approach.* Edmonton: University of Alberta Press, 1987.

Plunkett, Thomas. *Urban Canada and Its Government: A Study of Municipal Organization.* Toronto: Macmillan, 1968.

Plunkett, T.J. *City Government in Canada: The Role of the Chief Administrative Officer.* Toronto: The Institute of Public Administration of Canada, 1992.

Richardson, Boyce. *The Future of Canadian Cities.* Toronto: New Press, 1972.

Rystrom, Kenneth. *The Why, Who and How of the Editorial Page.* New York: Random House, 1983.

Sarpkaya, S. *Lobbying in Canada: Ways and Means.* Don Mills: CCH Canadian, 1988.

Seidle, F. Leslie (ed). *Interest Groups and Elections in Canada, Vol. 2.* Toronto: Dundurn Press, 1991.

Smith, Donald B. (ed). *Centennial City: Calgary 1894 to 1994.* Calgary: University of Calgary, 1994.

Toynbee, Arnold. *The Greeks and Their Heritages.* Oxford: Oxford University Press, 1981.

Weihs, Jean. *Facts about Canada, Its Provinces and Territories.* New York: H.W. Wilson, 1995.

Wood, Jonina (ed). *Canadian Yearbook 1994.* Ottawa: Statistics Canada, 1994.

Wood, Michael. *Legacy: The Search for Ancient Cultures.* New York: Sterling, 1992.

Wu, K.C. *The Chinese Heritage.* New York: Crown Publishers, 1982.

Glossary

acclamation –*n.* election without opposition; a public office won because there was no competition

administer –*v.* to manage and supervise local affairs

administration –*n.* the management and supervision of local affairs by government officials

advocacy –*n.* active support of an idea, cause, or policy, such as rights for people with disabilities

affirming –*v.* showing or demonstrating support

agenda –*n.* a list of things to be discussed

amalgamate –*v.* to combine two or more things, such as municipalities, into one

ancestor –*n.* a grandparent, great-grandparent, or forebear

annually –*adv.* once a year

archive –*n.* a library or storehouse for historical information

aristocracy –*n.* nobility, people who inherit highly-ranked positions in the community

awareness –*n.* to know or realize

ballot –*n.* the official piece of paper used in voting

baptized –*v.* to be named in a religious ceremony; to become part of a religious community

bilingual –*adj.* able to speak in two languages

bill –*n.* a draft of a proposed law presented for approval by a legislative body

borough –*n.* another name for a town or city that has its own local government

by-law –*n.* a law made by a local government

census –*n.* an official count of the people in the community

civil service –*n.* people directly employed by government to provide services

classify –*v.* to arrange according to characteristics

code of conduct –*n.* a collection of rules or laws about how to behave

colony –*n.* a settlement of people in a new land some distance from their home community

commissioner –*n.* a representative in charge

compensation –*n.* something given as repayment for a loss

Confederation –*n.* an official joining together of governments

confluence –*n.* the place where two or more rivers join and flow together

constituency –*n.* a district (area) represented by members of a lawmaking body; a riding

constitution –*n.* the rules and beliefs which guide the work of government

corrupt –*adj.* a way of behaving that is dishonest or deceitful

council –*n.* a group or special committee that gives advice

crusade –*n.* a vigorous movement for a cause

cul-de-sac –*n.* a dead end street

currency –*n.* any form of money

debate –*v.* to discuss the arguments for and against an issue

democracy –*n.* a form of government that is elected and controlled by the people who live under it

descendant –*n.* child, grandchild, great-grandchild, and so on

despotism –*n.* dictatorship; one person or one party rule

dignitaries –*n.* important or famous people

direct democracy –*n.* a form of government in which people govern themselves, making the laws for their community together

discriminated against *–v.* isolated, treated unfairly

district *–n.* a part of a region

Dominion *–n.* a self-governing nation within the British Commonwealth

dynasty *–n.* a series of rulers belonging to the same family

economy *–n.* the management of the resources of a country, community, or business

elected *–adj.* a person chosen in a vote

eligible *–adj.* being qualified, acceptable, able to be chosen

employment *–n.* the work a person is paid to do

empowered *–v.* to be given power

enacts *–v.* makes into law

enfranchise *–v.* to give the right to participate

ensure *–v.* to guarantee or make something happen

entrusted *–v.* to be counted on or believed in

enumeration list *–n.* official list of eligible voters

enumerators *–n.* people who compile lists of eligible voters

exploitation *–n.* the act of using other people for selfish reasons

federal *–adj.* a form of government; the central government in Canada

federation *–n.* a league or union of groups

feudalism *–n.* a system of governing based on land use in exchange for service; feudalism existed from the 800s to 1400s in Europe

gender *–n.* sex; male or female

hospitality *–n.* friendly treatment

House of Commons *–n.* the elected Members of Parliament in the federal government

image *–n.* an appearance or impression

immigrant *–n.* a person who has come to a new country to live

incorporated *–adj.* officially a community established under provincial or territorial law

incumbent *–n.* the person who presently is holding the office

infraction *–n.* a breaking of a law

integrity *–n.* honesty, self respect

interdependent *–adj.* dependent or reliant on one another

interpret *–v.* to explain or translate; to apply (a law)

judiciary *–n.* a system of courts

justice *–n.* the administration and process of the law

legislative *–adj.* having the power to make laws

liable *–adj.* to be responsible by law

lieutenant-governor *–n.* representative of the monarchy in the provinces

lobby group *–n.* a group of people who try to influence political decisions

loyal *–adj.* being dependable and faithful

majority *–n.* more than half; those who are in the greater number

maritime *–adj.* located by the sea

media *–n.* means of mass communication, such as radio, newspapers, television, billboards

metropolitan *–adj.* a major city and its suburbs; a form of local government based on several municipalities joining together to form a large urban area

minority *–n.* less than half; those who are out-numbered

monarchy *–n.* government by a sovereign, such as a king or queen

moratorium *–n.* an official delay

municipal –*adj.* local, community level of government

negotiate –*v.* to try to reach an agreement through discussion

office –*n.* in politics, a political position, such as a city councillor

Official Opposition –*n.* the second largest group of elected members of government who debate about the plans and actions of the political party or government in power

opponents –*n.* people with the opposite point-of-view

ordained –*v.* to be appointed to an official position

ordinance –*n.* a rule or law made by authority

parliament –*n.* assembly of representatives; a legislative (lawmaking) body; Canada's Parliament today is the federal lawmaking body consisting of the House of Commons (elected) and the Senate (appointed)

petition –*n.* a formal request to government which has been signed by many people

platforms –*n.* the promised action plans of political candidates

plebiscite –*n.* a vote taken on an issue among all citizens

policies –*n.* plans of action

portfolio –*n.* specific responsibilities assigned to a member of government

power –*n.* the authority to do a job or make a decision; the ability to control

probationary –*adj.* having to do with a trial or test period

psychological –*adj.* having to do with the mind

qualifications –*n.* the characteristics or skills that make a person suitable for a job

reeve –*n.* an elected community leader in a rural area

regulations –*n.* laws or rules

repeal –*v.* to cancel or do away with

representative democracy –*n.* a style of government in which voters elect people to speak on their behalf

representatives –*n.* those chosen to act or speak for others

responsible –*adj.* answerable to the people or their representatives

returning officer –*n.* the person who conducts an election locally and reports its results officially

riding –*n.* a district (area) represented by members of a lawmaking body; a constituency

right –*n.* something that is owed to a person by law, tradition, or nature

rural –*adj.* in the country

sanitarium –*n.* a hospital for resting and healing

social –*adj.* having to do with being part of a community

society –*n.* an organized human grouping, community

status –*n.* recognized standing or position in a community; official recognition

subsidize –*v.* to assist, or to support with money

summary conviction –*n.* a quick judgment

town hall meeting –*n.* an open meeting of citizens in which government representatives give information, and citizens voice their ideas and opinions

township –*n.* a unit of government in central Canada; a survey unit of land on Canada's prairies

uphold –*v.* to agree with and enforce

urban –*adj.* in the city

virtuous –*adj.* a way of behaving that is valued

Index

FC 34.44

Photo Credits

Entries
are by page number, coded as follows:

T=Top   B=Bottom   M=Middle
L=Left   R=Right

Abbreviations:
GNWT EC & E –Government of the Northwest Territories Education, Culture and Employment
NAC –National Archives of Canada
PAA –Provincial Archives of Alberta

Front Cover:
TL   Doctor and patient, Photo by Emir Poelzer, Royal Alexandra Hospital
TM   Hutterite women in truck, CANAPRESS / Colin Corneau
TR   Earl of Durham, NAC C5456
ML   Nellie McClung, PAA A3354
MM   Demonstration, CANAPRESS / Moe Doiron
MR   Inuit man, 1995-001 Tessa Macintosh / NWT Archives / GNWT EC & E
BL   Mayor Frank Faubert of Scarborough, CANAPRESS / Frank Gunn
BM   Canadian Citizenship Ceremony, CANAPRESS / Jacques Boissinot

Back Cover:
MM   Demonstration, CANAPRESS / Moe Doiron

Page:
1   PAA A2216
2   (TR) PAA B3999
2   (TL) PAA BL.34/2
2   (B) PAA A2216
10   PAA A13,986
12   Rogers Cantel Inc.
19   NAC C5456
20   Rogers Cantel Inc.
24   PAA B3955
25   Photo by Emir Poelzer, Royal Alexandra Hospital
26   (T) Habitat for Humanity, Edmonton
26   (B) Edmonton's Food Bank
27   Photo by Emir Poelzer, Royal Alexandra Hospital
29   Courtesy of Ford Motor Company
30   (L) James Steeves, Atlantic Stock Images Inc.
30   (R) Tourism Saskatchewan
30   (B) Reidmore Books
32   Tourism British Columbia.
33   CANAPRESS / Joe Gibbons
36   Courtesy of the Canadian Tourism Commission
39   Courtesy of the Canadian Tourism Commission
40   Don Hall, University of Regina
41   Fran Hurcomb / NWT Archives / GNWT EC & E
43   Frank Grant, GNWT, Yellowknife
44   Fredericton Tourism
46   Frank Grant, GNWT, Yellowknife
47   Saint John (NB) Visitor and Convention Bureau
49   Canadian Olympic Association
50   PAA A2293
51   Photo by Albert Lee
51   PAA C147
52   (L) Warren Gordon
52   (R) Yukon Archives / National Museum of Canada Collection
53   (L) The St. Lawrence Seaway Authority

53   (R) Michael Jessop, Studio Laporte
54   (L) Photo by Albert Lee
54   (TR) Photo by Albert Lee
54   (BR) Reidmore Books
55   Photo B292 by Leonard Hillyard. Courtesy of Saskatoon Public Library—Local History Room
58   Gerald Vander Pyl, Calgary Convention and Visitors Bureau
60   G-1995-001 Tessa Macintosh / NWT Archives / GNWT EC & E
61   CANAPRESS/Frank Gunn
64   CANAPRESS/Dave Buston
67   PAA A4520
68   CANAPRESS / Colin Corneau
69   British Columbia Film Commission / Small Business, Tourism & Culture
71   G-1995-001 Tessa Macintosh / NWT Archives / GNWT EC & E
73   CANAPRESS / Moe Doiron
74   CANAPRESS / Jeff McIntosh
76   Bruce Fleming
77   CANAPRESS / Fred Chartrand
78   English Express / Alberta Advanced Education and Career Development
79   CANAPRESS / Jeff McIntosh
80   CANAPRESS / Jeff McIntosh
81   Bruce Fleming
82   English Express / Alberta Advanced Education and Career Development
83   CANAPRESS / Jacques Boissinot
85   CANAPRESS / Randy Fiedler
86   CANAPRESS / Moe Doiron
87   CANAPRESS / Jeff McIntosh
93   PAA P129

We have made every effort to correctly identify and credit the sources of all photographs, illustrations, and information used in this textbook. Reidmore Books appreciates any further information or corrections; acknowledgement will be given in subsequent editions.